Everybody's
Favorite
Series No. 5

Trade Mark

SONGS
FOR
CHILDREN

FOREWORD Songs for Children *is dedicated to children everywhere. It was inspired by "The Lady of the Moon", a youngster who came to me every day for months so that I might tell her a story about her nursery rhymes and teach her new games.*

To "The Lady of the Moon" then I offer this book as my testimony that I, too, derived pleasure from her daily visits, her childish amusement and wonder as I unfolded the tales and played the songs contained herein.

To her, and the millions just like her, I offer it hoping that everyone everywhere gets the same enjoyment from it as my "Lady of the Moon" and one who she called "The Lamplighter"--

W. J. GLASSMACHER, EDITOR

Arrangements for piano by Robert S. Keller

International Standard Book Number: 0-8256-2005-8

Distributed throughout the world by Music Sales Corporation:

33 West 60th Street, New York 10023
78 Newman Street, London W1P 3LA
27 Clarendon Street, Artarmon, Sydney NSW 2064
Kölner Strasse 199, D-5000, Cologne 90

SONGS FOR CHILDREN

CLASSIFIED INDEX

EVERYBODY'S FAVORITE SERIES No. 5
SONGS FOR CHILDREN

CONTENTS

WELCOME SWEET SPRING

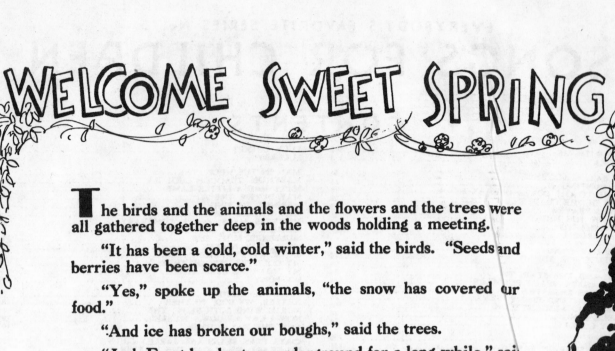

The birds and the animals and the flowers and the trees were all gathered together deep in the woods holding a meeting.

"It has been a cold, cold winter," said the birds. "Seeds and berries have been scarce."

"Yes," spoke up the animals, "the snow has covered our food."

"And ice has broken our boughs," said the trees.

"Jack Frost has kept us underground for a long while," said the flowers.

A wise old owl, who was their chosen leader, listened to their stories, and at last rapped on the stump of the hollow tree that was acting as his desk. "Friends of nature," he said, "our neighbor, the groundhog, tells me that winter has at last fled, and that tomorrow at dawn the Queen of Spring will come to rule our kingdom. How shall we greet her?"

"We will dress in our new blossoms," said the violets.

"And we will wear our white bonnets," said the mayflowers.

"And we will deck our branches with green buds," the trees said.

"And we will all sing our sweetest songs," said the birds.

And so all the flowers, the trees, the animals and birds joined together for a grand reception to greet the Queen of Spring. And swiftly, at the first blush of dawn the wise old owl gave the signal—a cricket band played and the birds welcomed the arrival of the sweetest season of all.

Welcome, Sweet Spring-Time !

A. Rubinstein

Wel - come, sweet Spring-time! We greet thee in song, Mur - murs of
Wel - come, sweet Spring-time! What joy now is ours, Win - ter has

glad - ness fall on the ear,— Voi - ces long hush'd, now their
fled to far dis - tant climes, Flow - ers thy pres - ence a -

full notes pro - long— E - cho-ing far and near.———
waits in the bow - ers Long - ing for thy first kiss.———

Spring, Gentle Spring

J. R. Planche

Spread thy robe of bright-est green, We will wel-come thee with

joy, We will wel-come thee with joy. Spring! Spring!

gen - tle Spring! Young-est sea-son of the year Life and

joy to na - ture bring: gen - tle, gen - tle, gen - tle Spring.

The Snow Man

Alfred S. Gatty

Quickly

Come out, dear Dol-ly and make a snow man, Ha! Ha! ev-er so big;
Run in, dear Dol-ly and bring pa-pa's hat, Ha! Ha! out of the hall;

You must work Dol-ly, as hard as you can, Ha! Ha! dig Dol-ly dig;
Oh, what a pi-ty, we've made him so fat, Ha! Ha! t'won't fit at all;

You get the snow, while I make the head, And pick me two stones for his eyes,
Oh, Dol-ly dear, how clum-sy you are, You've knock'd a great hole in the side of

We'll try and make him like Un-cle Ned, To take dear pa-pa by sur-prise;
fa-ther's new hat, and here comes ma-ma, So Dol-ly lets run and hide;

Jolly Old Saint Nicholas

When the clock is strik-ing twelve, When I'm fast a-sleep, Down the chim-ney,

broad and black, With your pack you'll creep; All the stock-ings you will find

Hang-ing in a row; Mine will be the short-est one; You'll be sure to know.

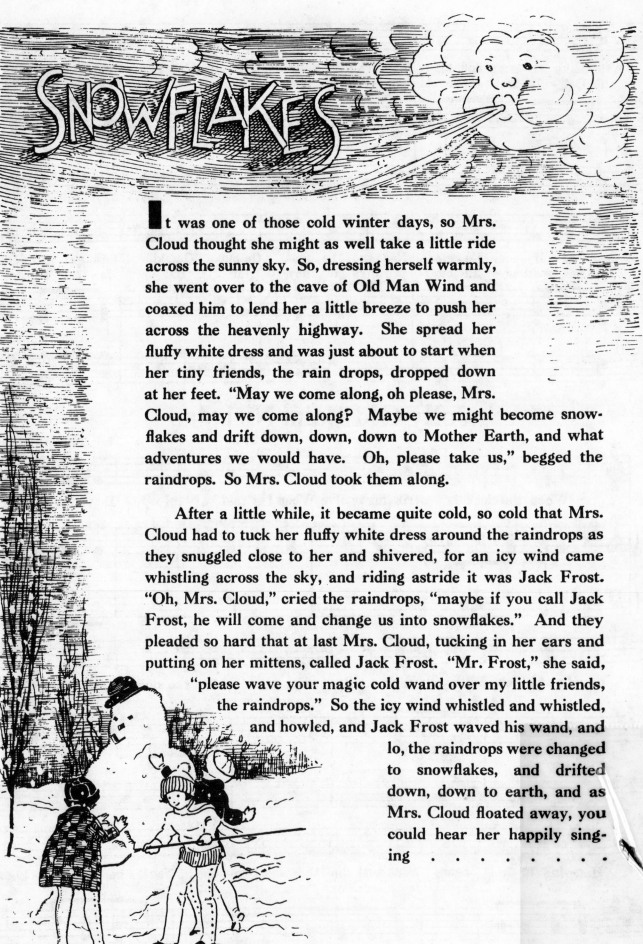

SNOWFLAKES

It was one of those cold winter days, so Mrs. Cloud thought she might as well take a little ride across the sunny sky. So, dressing herself warmly, she went over to the cave of Old Man Wind and coaxed him to lend her a little breeze to push her across the heavenly highway. She spread her fluffy white dress and was just about to start when her tiny friends, the rain drops, dropped down at her feet. "May we come along, oh please, Mrs. Cloud, may we come along? Maybe we might become snowflakes and drift down, down, down to Mother Earth, and what adventures we would have. Oh, please take us," begged the raindrops. So Mrs. Cloud took them along.

After a little while, it became quite cold, so cold that Mrs. Cloud had to tuck her fluffy white dress around the raindrops as they snuggled close to her and shivered, for an icy wind came whistling across the sky, and riding astride it was Jack Frost. "Oh, Mrs. Cloud," cried the raindrops, "maybe if you call Jack Frost, he will come and change us into snowflakes." And they pleaded so hard that at last Mrs. Cloud, tucking in her ears and putting on her mittens, called Jack Frost. "Mr. Frost," she said, "please wave your magic cold wand over my little friends, the raindrops." So the icy wind whistled and whistled, and howled, and Jack Frost waved his wand, and lo, the raindrops were changed to snowflakes, and drifted down, down to earth, and as Mrs. Cloud floated away, you could hear her happily singing . . . .

Barbelle

Snow Flakes

Mary Mapes Dodge

Frederick H. Cowen

thee. Thou art so bare and lone-ly, dear, Thou art so bare and lone-ly

dear. I'll rest, and call my com-rades here." But when a

snow - flake, brave and meek, Lights on a lit - tle maid-en's cheek. It starts —

"how warm and soft the day, how warm and

soft the day, 'Tis sum-mer, 'tis sum-mer, 'tis sum -

mer." And it melts a - way.

The North Wind Doth Blow

J. W. Elliott

The North wind doth blow, And we shall have snow, And what will poor rob-in do then? He'll

sit in the barn, And keep him-self warm, And tuck his head un-der his wing, poor thing!

JINGLE BELLS

"Look out of the window," said Dobbin, the horse, "There are snow-flakes dancing past."

"Well, well," said the old sleigh, as it tried to shake the dust off itself, "It's the first snow storm, and I guess we'll be out for a ride in the morning. My, it will be good to be out again. My runners are a bit rusty, but I'll shine them up as soon as I get out; but where are my bells?"

"Oh, they are at school, learning to sing clear and sweet," said Dobbin. "You know, just any old bell cannot sing on a sleigh. It would seem funny to have the bells that sing on the cow, or the big bells with the loud song that sing in the church tower, or even the dinner bell try to sing for a sleigh. It takes a special song, clear and bright and happy. Why, Mr. Sleigh, here come your bells now. Listen to their song of winter and snow."

Jingle Bells

Dash-ing through the snow, In a one-horse o-pen sleigh; While o'er the fields we go, Laugh-ing all the way; Bells on bob-tail ring, Mak-ing spir-its bright, What fun it is to ride and sing a-sleigh-ing song to-night. Jin-gle bells! Jin-gle bells! Jin-gle all the way Oh! what fun it is to ride in a

Three Children Sliding

Calendar Song

Six - ty sec-onds make a min - ute, Some-thing sure you can learn in it;
Fif - ty-two weeks make a year, Soon a new one will be here;
Twen-ty-eight is all his share, With twen-ty nine in each leap year;

Six - ty min-utes make an hour, Work with all your might and pow'r,
Twelve long months a year will make, Say them now with - out mis - take,
That you may the Leap-year know, Di - vide by four and that will show,

Twen - ty-four hours make a day, Time e - nough for work and play,
Thir - ty days hath gay Sep - tem-ber, A - pril, June and cold No - vem-ber;
In each year are sea - sons four, You will learn them I am sure;

Sev - en days a week will make; You will learn if pains you take.
All the rest have thir - ty - one; Feb - u - a - ry stands a - lone.
Spring and Sum-mer, then the Fall; Win - ter, last, but best of all.

Rain Upon The Roof

When the hu-mid show-ers gath-er O-ver all the star-ry spheres,

And the mel-an-cho-ly dark-ness Gen-tly weeps in rain-y tears.'Tis a

joy to press the pil-low, Of a cot-tage cham-ber bed, And to

lis-ten to the pat-ter, Of the soft rain o-ver-head_____ And to

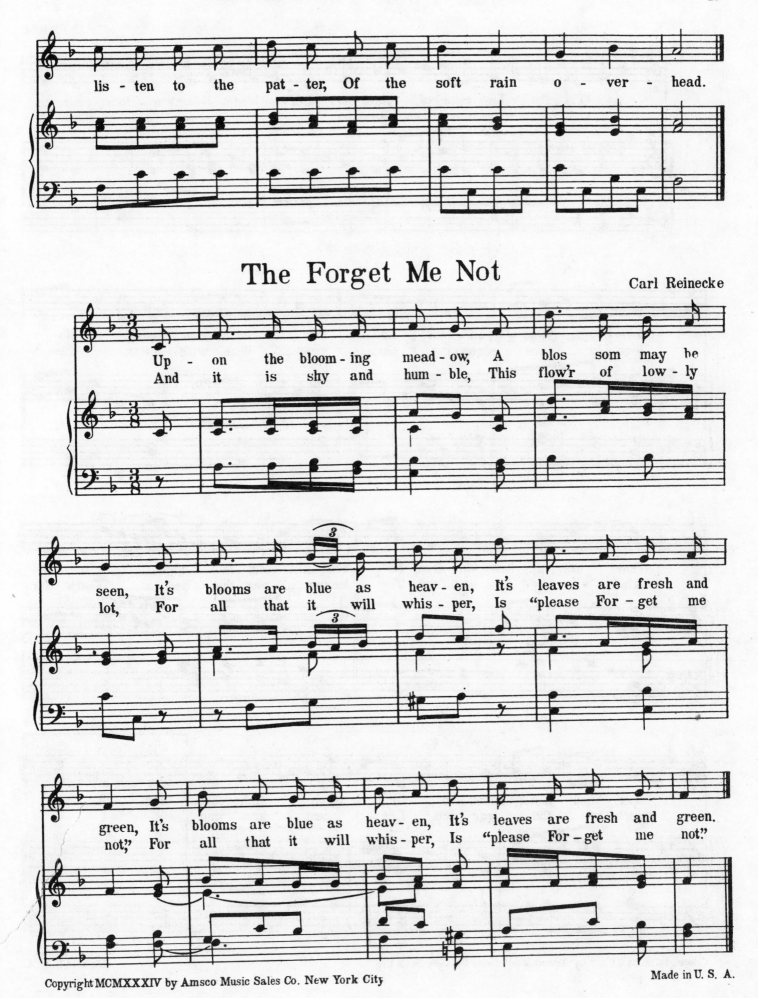

The Forget Me Not

Carl Reinecke

The Last Rose Of Summer

F. Flotow

dead Where thy mates of __ the gar-den Lie__ scent - less and dead.

Twinkle, Twinkle Little Star

Twin-kle twin-kle lit - tle star; How I won-der what you are,
When the blaz-ing sun is gone; When he noth-ing shines up - on,

Up a - bove the world so high, Like a dia - mond in the sky!
Then you show your lit - tle light, Twin-kle twin-kle all the night!

Twin-kle twin-kle lit - tle star, How I won-der what you are!

Made in U.S.A.

A Frog He Would A-Wooing Go

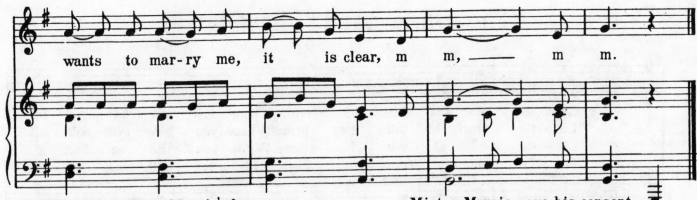

wants to mar-ry me, it is clear, m m, —— m m.

2. He rode right to Miss Mousie's den, m-m-m-m
He rode right to Miss Mousie's den, m-m-m-m
Said he Miss Mousie are you within m-m-m-m

3 "Oh yes kind sir, I sit and spin,
Oh yes kind sir, I sit and spin,
Lift the latch and walk right in."

4 He said "Miss Mouse I've come to see"
He said "Miss Mouse I've come to see"
If you, Miss Mousie, will you marry me?

5 Oh as for that I cannot say
Oh as for that I cannot say
For Mister Mousie has gone away.

6 Mister Mousie gave his consent
Mister Mousie gave his consent
And the weasel wrote the publishment.

7 Where shall the wedding supper be
Where shall the wedding supper be
Way down yonder in a hollow tree.

8 The first that came was a bumble bee
The first that came was a bumble bee,
Carrying a fiddle on his knee.

9 The next that came was a big black bug
The next that came was a big black bug,
On his back was a water jug.

10 Bread and butter lie on the shelf,
Bread and butter lie on the shelf,
If you want more sing it your self.

The Seasons

I love the Spring, when sleep-ing birds Are wak-ened un-to birth, When
I love the Sum-mer, when the flow'rs Look beau-ti-ful and bright, When
I love the Au-tumn, when the trees, With fruit are bend-ing low, When
I love to have the Win-ter come, When I can skate and slide, And

joy and glad-ness seem to spread, At once o'er all the earth.
I can play and romp for hours, With hoop and ball and kite.
I can reach the pears and plums, That hang up-on the bough.
hear the bells and see the sleighs, That swift-ly by us glide.

Made in U. S. A.

24

The Child And The Star

Slowly

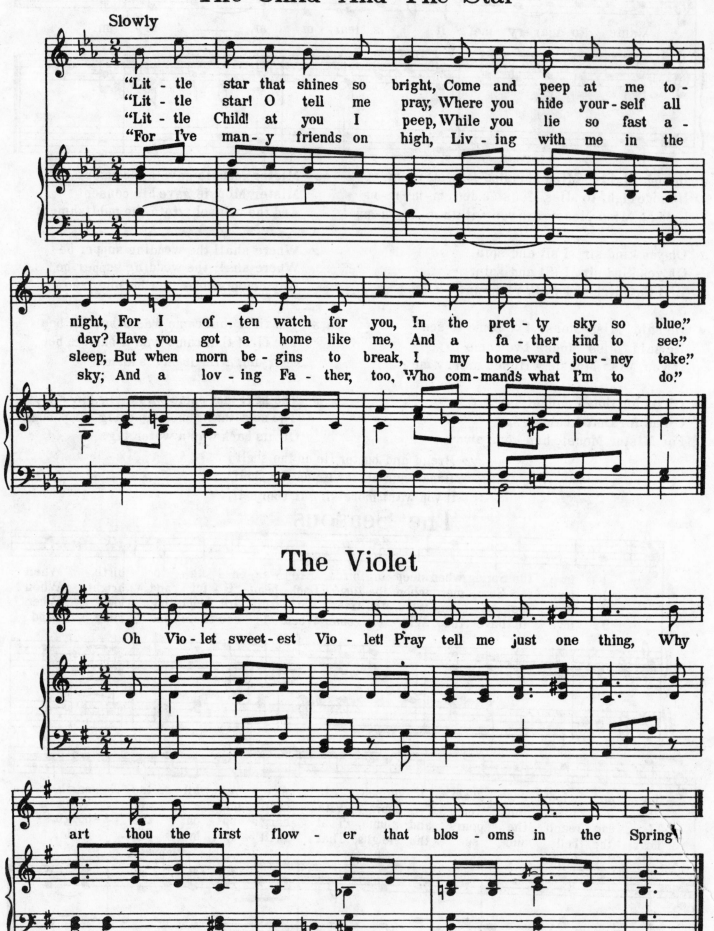

"Lit - tle star that shines so bright, Come and peep at me to-
"Lit - tle star! O tell me pray, Where you hide your-self all
"Lit - tle Child! at you I peep, While you lie so fast a-
"For I've man - y friends on high, Liv - ing with me in the

night, For I of - ten watch for you, In the pret - ty sky so blue."
day? Have you got a home like me, And a fa - ther kind to see."
sleep; But when morn be - gins to break, I my home-ward jour - ney take."
sky; And a lov - ing Fa - ther, too, Who com-mands what I'm to do."

The Violet

Oh Vio - let sweet - est Vio - let! Pray tell me just one thing, Why

art thou the first flow - er that blos - oms in the Spring

Made in U. S. A.

ROBIN SING FOR ME

Raka Waga

Cock Robin And Jenny Wren

'Twas in a mer-ry time, When Jen-ny Wren was young, So neat-ly as she
My dear-est Jen-ny Wren, If you will but be mine, You shall dine on cher-ry

danc'd And so sweet-ly as she sung, Rob-in Red-breast lost his heart, He
pie, And drink nice cur-rant wine; I'll dress you like a gold-finch Or

was a gal-lant bird, He doff'd his cap to Jen-ny Wren, re-quest-ing to be heard.
like a pea-cock gay, So if you'll have me Jen-ny Wren, Let us ap-point the day.

3 Jenny blush'd behind her fan and thus declared her mind:
"So let it be to-morrow, Rob, I'll take your offer kind;
Cherry pie is very good and so is currant wine,
But I will wear my plain brown gown, and never dress up fine.

4 Robin Redbreast got up early, all at the break of day,
He flew to Jenny Wren's house, and sang a roundelay;
He sang of Robin Redbreast and pretty Jenny Wren,
And when he came unto the end, he then began again.

Made in U.S.A.

To The Nightingale

Carl Reinecke

Sing for us sweet songs-tress, love-ly night-in-gale,

Send thy song re - sound-ing O - ver hill and dale!

Send thy song re - sound-ing O - ver hill and dale!

Tra li tra la, tra li tra la, tra li, tra la, tra li, tra la.

Made in U. S. A.

Birds In The Night

Gently

Arthur Sullivan

Birds in the night that soft-ly call, Winds in the night that
Life may be sad for us that wake, Sleep lit-tle bird, and

strong-ly sigh, Come to me, help me, one and all, To
dream not why; Soon is the sleep but God can break, When

sing soft-ly ba-by's lul-la-by, Lul-la-by, Lul-la-by, Lul-la
an-gels whis-per lul-la-by,

lul-la lul-la lul-la lul-la-by, Lul-la-by baby, While the ho-urs run,

Made in U.S.A.

Fair may the day be when night is done, Lul - la - by, ba - by, While the hours run, Lul - la -

by, lul - la - by, lul - la - by, lul - la - by, lul - la - by, lul - la - by.

Birdie In The Cradle

Franz Abt

In the tall boughs on the tree top there's a nest so sung and warm; In it lies a lit-tle
At eve bird - ie's gen-tle moth-er hov - ers o'er the co - zy nest, Warb-ling, sing-ing, oh, so

bird-ie Safe in sun-shine, safe in storm; In it lies a lit-tle bird - ie, safe in sun-shine, safe in storm.
sweet-ly! Till her loved one is at rest; Warb-ling, sing-ing, oh, so sweet-ly! Till her loved one is at rest.

Made in U.S.A.

THREE LITTLE KITTENS

"Miew, miew," said Mrs. Pussy Cat to her kittens, "I don't know what I'll ever do to make you children behave. Where is the catnip I sent to the store for, and where, oh where, is the mouse that was to be caught for supper? And what about the milk that the cow promised? Dear me, here I've been all day, knitting and knitting and knitting, and I'm almost afraid to give you your presents that I've made. You know, children, soon it will be getting very cold and Jack Frost will bring ice and snow."

"Miew, miew," said one little kitten, "here is the catnip, mother dear. I forgot to tell you I brought it."

"Miew, miew," said the other little kitten. "I caught two mice and here they are, mother dear," said the other little kitten."

"Well, well," said Mrs. Pussy Cat, "You have been good little kittens. Look, here are your presents—warm, knitted mittens. But be careful of them. You know what will happen if you lose them. Gather close around me and I will tell you."

Three Little Kittens

Mi - ew,　Mi - ew,　Mi - ew,　Mi - ew,　Mi - ew.

Three Little Mice

Three lit - tle mice crept out　to see What they could find to　have for tea, for

they were dain - ty,　sau - cy mice, And lik'd to nib - ble some-thing nice, But

Pus - sy's eyes, so　big and bright, Soon sent them scamper-ing　off in a fright.

slower

a tempo

Made in U. S. A.

I Love Little Pussy

I love lit-tle pus-sy, her coat is so warm, And if I don't hurt her she'll do me no harm, So I'll not pull her tail nor drive her a-way, But pus-sy and I— to geth-er will play.

The Lazy Cat

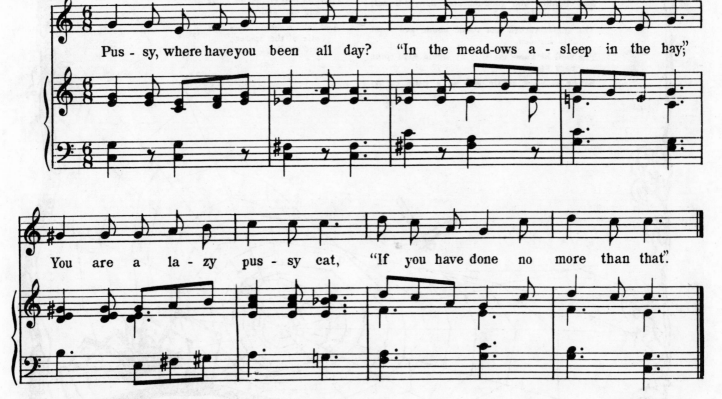

Pus-sy, where have you been all day? "In the mead-ows a-sleep in the hay;" You are a la-zy pus-sy cat, "If you have done no more than that".

Made in U. S. A.

THE SPIDER AND THE FLY

"Will you walk into my parlor?" said the
spider to the fly;

"'Tis the prettiest little parlor that ever you
did spy.

The way into my parlor is up a winding
stair;

And I have many curious things to show you
when you're there."

"Oh, no, no," said the little fly; "to ask me is
in vain;

For who goes up your winding stair can ne'er
come down again."

"I'm sure you must be weary, dear, with soaring
up so high;

Will you rest upon my little bed?" said the
spider to the fly.

"There are pretty curtains drawn around; the
sheets are fine and thin;

And if you like to rest awhile, I'll snugly tuck
you in!"

"Oh, no, no," said the little fly; "for I've often
heard it said,

They never, never wake again, who sleep upon
your bed!"

Said the cunning spider to the fly,—"Dear friend,
what can I do

To prove the warm affection I've always felt
for you?"

"I thank you, gentle sir," she said, "for what
you're pleased to say,

And bidding you good-morning now, I'll call
another day."

The spider turned him round about, and went
into his den,

For well he knew the silly fly would soon come
back again;

So he wove a subtle web in a little corner
sly,

And set his table ready, to dine upon the
fly.

Then he came out to his door again, and merrily
did sing,—

"Come hither, hither, pretty fly, with the pearl
and silver wing;

Your robes are green and purple—there's a crest
upon your head!

Your eyes are like the diamond bright, but mine
are dull as lead!"

Alas, alas! how very soon this silly little
fly,

Hearing his wily, flattering words, came slowly
flitting by.

With buzzing wings she hung aloft, then near
and nearer drew.

Thinking only of her brilliant eyes, her green
and purple hue—

Thinking only of her crested head—poor foolish
thing! At last,

Up jumped the cunning spider, and fiercely held
her fast!

He dragged her up his winding stair, into his
dismal den,

Within his little parlor—but she ne'er came
out again!

And now, dear little children, who may
this story read,

To idle, silly, flattering words, I pray
you ne'er give heed;

Unto an evil counselor close heart,
and ear, and eye,

And take a lesson from this
tale of the Spider
and the Fly.

The Spider And The Fly

Raka Waga

Will you walk in-to my par-lor, said the Spid-er to the Fly "Tis the pret-ti-est lit-tle
Will you walk in-to my par-lor, said the Spid-er to the Fly "I've the lov-li-est lit-tle

par-lor that ev-er you did spy" If you'll on-ly take a lit-tle peek just in-side the
ham-mock that ev-er you did try" If you'll on-ly just come in a while I know you'll want to

door, "You'll see some ver-y cu-ri-ous things you nev-er saw be-fore" Oh, will you, will you,
stay, "You'll love my pret-ty sil-ver-y web you'll nev er go a-way"

will you, will you, walk in, mis-ter fly? Oh will you, will you will you, will you walk in mis-ter fly.

Made in U.S.A.

The Dog And Cat

Why do you scratch me Puss - y, You naugh - ty lit - tle thing? Un-
Dear Ro-ver you must stroke me, And praise my fur so white! Must
But Ro-ver said to Kit - ty, There is no truth in that, Al-

less you stop, Miss Pus - sy, An - oth - er tune you'll sing! So
pet me and ca - ress me, For that is my de - light. I
though you purr so gen - tly, One can't be-lieve a cat I'm

Ro - ver said to Kit - ty, And looked quite cross at her; But
am not cross, be - lieve me, Each word I say is true; I
grieved to say, Miss Puss - y You I can nev - er trust! I

in her gen - tlest man - ner, Miss Puss be - gan to purr. Me-
on - ly purr and mur - mur, Be - cause I'm fond of you. Me-
know your claws are cru - el, And run a - way I must. Bow-

Made in U.S.A.

ow, me-ow, me-ow, me-ow, Miss Puss be-gan to purr, Me-
ow, me-ow, me-ow, me-ow, Be-cause I'm fond of you, Me-
wow, bow-wow, bow-wow, bow-wow, Now run a-way I must, Bow-

ow, me-ow, me-ow, me-ow, Miss Puss be-gan to purr.
ow, me-ow, me-ow, me-ow, Be-cause I'm fond of you.
wow, bow-wow, bow-wow, bow-wow, Now run a-way I must.

Johnny Had A Little Dog

John-ny had a lit-tle dog, and Bin-go was his name, sir B-I-N-G-O go

B-I-N-G-O go, B-I-N-G-O go, Bin-go was his name, sir.

POOR COCK ROBIN

Who killed Cock Robin?
"I," said the sparrow,
"With my little bow and arrow,
I killed Cock Robin."

Who saw him die?
"I," said the fly,
"With my little eye,
I saw him die."

Who'll make his shroud?
"I," said the beetle,
"With my thread and needle,
"I'll make his shroud."

Who'll carry the torch?
"I," said the linnet,
"I'll come in a minute,
I'll carry the torch."

Who'll be the clerk?
"I," said the lark,
"If it's not in the dark,
I'll be the clerk."

Who'll dig his grave?
"I," said the owl,
"With my spade and trowel,
I'll dig his grave."

Who'll be the parson?
"I," said the rook,
"With my little book,
I'll be the parson."

Who'll be the chief mourner?
"I," said the dove,
"I mourn for my love,
I'll be chief mourner."

Who'll sing a psalm?
"I," said the thrush,
"As I sit in the bush,
I'll sing a psalm."

Who'll carry the coffin?
"I," said the kite,
"If it's not in the night,
I'll carry the coffin."

Who'll toll the bell?
"I," said the bull,
Because I can pull,
I'll toll the bell."

All the birds of the air
Fell sighing and sobbing,
When they heard the bell toll
For poor Cock Robin.

Who Killed Cock Robin

J. W. Elliott

Who kill'd Cock Ro-bin? I said the Spar-row, "With my bow and ar-row

I kill'd Cock Ro-bin" Who saw him die? "I" said the Fly "With

slower

my lit-tle eye I saw him die" Who caught his blood? "I" said the Fish,"With

a tempo

my lit-tle dish I caught his blood" Who'll make his shroud? I said the Beet-le,"With

Made in U S.A.

my thread and needle   I'll make his shroud"   Who'll bear the torch? "I" said the Lin net "Will

come in a min-ute;   Who'll be the clerk?   "I" said the Lark.

"I" said the Lark   "I'll say A-men in the dark;   I'll be the

clerk."   Who'll dig his grave? "I said the Owl; With my spade and trowl

I'll dig his grave" Who'll be the Par - son?

"I" said the Rock; With my lit-tle book I'll be the Par - son Who'll be chief mour-ner?

I said the Dove; "I mourn for my love I'll be chief mourner" Who'll sing his

dirge? "I" said the Thrush as I sing in a bush, "I'll sing his dirge"

Who'll car-ry his cof-fin I said the Kite; If it be in the

night, I'll car-ry his cof-fin. Who'll toll the bell?

"I" said the Bull "Be-cause I can pull, I'll toll the bell" All the birds of the air fell

lento

sigh-ing and sob-bing When they heard the bell toll For poor Cock Rob - in.

Sweet And Low

Alfred Tennyson

Sir Joseph Barnby

Sweet and low, sweet and low, Wind of the west - ern sea; Low, low,
Sleep and rest, sleep and rest, Fa-ther will come to thee soon; Rest, rest on

breathe and blow, Wind of the west - ern sea; O - ver the roll - ing
moth - er's breast, Fa-ther will come to thee soon; Fa-ther will come to his

wa - ters go, Come from the dy - ing moon and blow, Blow him a-gain to
babe in the nest, Sil - ver sails all out of the west, Un-der the sil - ver

me, While my lit - tle one, While my pret - ty one sleeps. _____
moon, Sleep my lit - tle one, Sleep my pret - ty one sleep. _____

Made in U. S. A.

Slumber Song

F. Kucken

All is still in sweet-est rest, Be thy sleep se - rene - ly
Close each lit - tle lov - ing eye, Let them like two rose - lets

blest! Winds are moan - ing o'er the wild, Lul - la - by sleep
lie; And when pur - pl'ing morn shall glow, Still as rose - lets

on my child; Lul - la - by sleep on my child, So lul - la -
fresh - ly blow; }

by sleep on my child; May an - gel gleams per - vade thy dreams.

Made in U. S. A.

Go To Sleep, Lena Darling

(Emmett's Lullaby)

J. K. Emmett

Close your eyes, Le - na, my dar - ling, While I sing your lul - la -
Bright be de morn - ing, my dar - ling, Ven you ope your eyes;

by, fear thou no dan - ger, Le - na, Move not, dear Le - na, my dar - ling, For your brooder watches
Sun beams glow all round you Le - na, Peace be with thee, love, my dar - ling, Blue and cloud less be the

nigh you, Le - na dear. An - gels guide thee, Le - na dear my dar - ling, Noth - ing e - vil
sky for, Le - na dear. Birds sing their bright songs for thee my dar - ling, Full of sweet - est

can come near, Bright - est flow - ers blow for thee, Dar - ling sis - ter,
mel - o - dy, An - gels ev - er hov - er near, Dar - ling sis - ter,

Made in U. S. A.

dear to me.   Go to sleep,   go to sleep my ba - by, my ba - by, my ba - by
dear to me.

Go to sleep, my ba - by,   ba - by, oh, bye!   Go to   leep, Le - na, sleep.

Cradle Song

C. M. Von Weber

Sleep my hearts dar - ling, in   slum - ber re - pose;   Let   the fair
Now dear - est   ba - by, it's   morn's gold - en   time;   Not   thus thoul't

lids o'er those blue eyes now   close;   All   is as   peace - ful and
slum - ber in   life's la - ter   prime;   Sor - row and   care then will

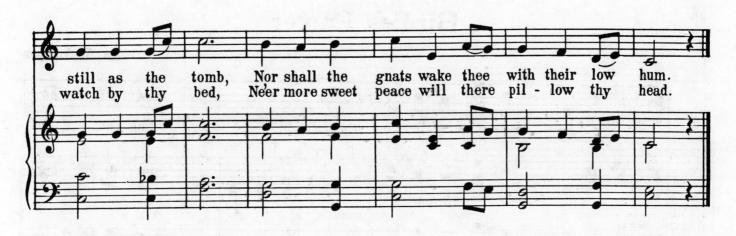

still as the tomb, Nor shall the gnats wake thee with their low hum.
watch by thy bed, Ne'er more sweet peace will there pil - low thy head.

When My Little Children Sleep

Carl Reinecke

When my lit-tle chil-dren sleep, Lit-tle stars are wak - ing, An-gels bright from

heav - en come, And, till dawn is break - ing, They will guard thee through the night

bring sweet dreams till morn-ing light, When my lit - tle chil - dren sleep, Stars and an - gels watch do keep.

Made in U.S.A.

Birdie's Prayer

A. T. Gorham

An - gels guard thy lit - tle bed ___ Dar - ling one, to-

night, Hov - er o'er thy sun - ny head. ___

Till the morn - ing light; Soft, while twi - light shad - ows

fall, ___ Now thy eye - lids close;

Made in U.S.A.

Calm 'neath mid-night's star-ry pall, _____ Be thy sweet re-
pose, Oh _____ an - gels guard thy lit - tle bed. _____
Dar - ling one to - night, Hov - er o'er thy sun - ny
head _____ Till the morn - ing light.

Sleep, Baby Sleep

German Folk Song

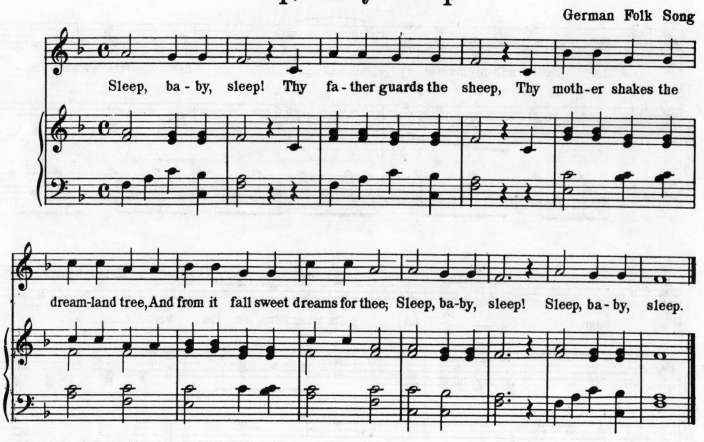

Rock-A-Bye Baby

Music by
MICHEL WHITEHILL

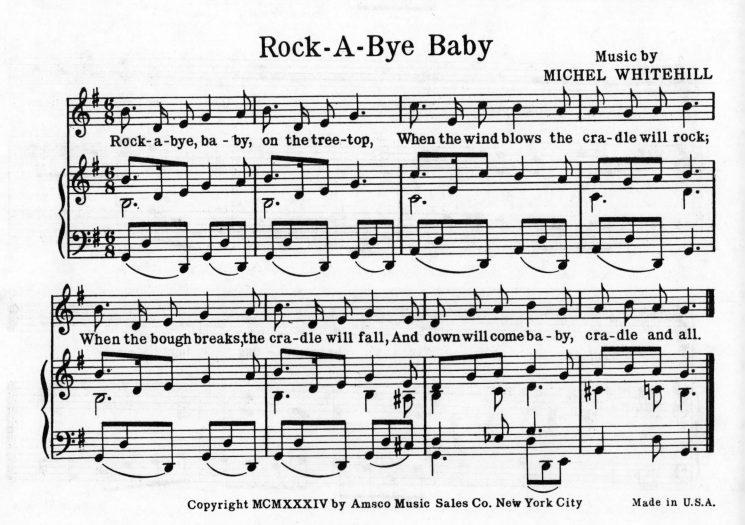

Winkum, Winkum

Wink - um, wink - um, shut your eyes, Sweet my ba - by's
Chick - ens long have gone to rest, Birds lie snug with -

lul - la - by, For the dews are fall - ing soft,
in their nest, And my bir - die soon will be,

Lights are flick' - ring up a - loft; And the moon - light's
Sleep - ing like a chic - a - dee; For with on - ly

peep - ing o - ver, yon - der hill - top capped with clov - er.
half a try Wink - um, wink - um, shut her eye.

The Little Cock Sparrow

Made in U.S.A.

chir-ripped, he chir-ripped, A lit - tle cock spar-row sat on a high tree, And he

chir-ripped, he chir-ripped so mer - ri - ly mer - ri - ly.

Tom, Tom, The Piper's Son

Tom, Tom, the pi-per's son, Stole a pig and a - way he run! The

pig was eat, And Tom was beat, Which sent him cry - ing down the street.

Made in U.S.A.

Baa! Baa! Black Sheep

Baa! Baa! Black sheep, have you an-y wool? Yes, sir, yes, sir! Three bags full,

One for my mast-er and one for my dame, But none for the lit-tle boy that cries in the lane.

Curly Locks

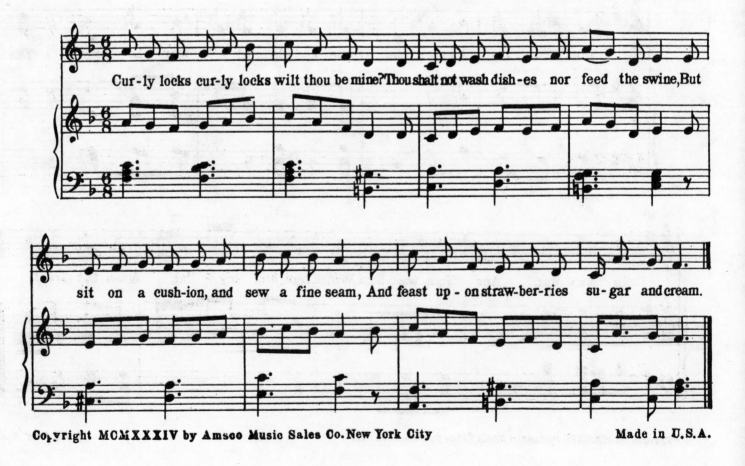

Cur-ly locks cur-ly locks wilt thou be mine? Thou shalt not wash dish-es nor feed the swine, But

sit on a cush-ion, and sew a fine seam, And feast up-on straw-ber-ries su-gar and cream.

 Made in U.S.A.

Mother, May I Go Out To Swim?

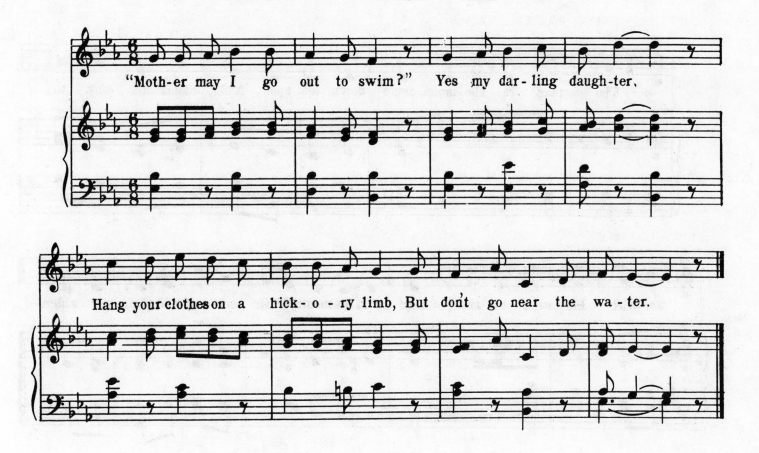

"Moth-er may I go out to swim?" Yes my dar-ling daugh-ter,

Hang your clothes on a hick-o-ry limb, But don't go near the wa-ter.

Natural History

What are lit-tle boys made of? What are lit-tle boys made of?
What are lit-tle girls made of? What are lit-tle girls made of?

Frogs and snakes and pup-py dog's tails, That's what lit-tle boys are made of.
Su-gar and spice and all that's nice, That's what lit-tle girls are made of.

Made in U. S. A.

The Man In The Moon

Mistress Mary, Quite Contrary

Made in U.S.A.

Bobby Shafto

Bob-by Shafto's gone to sea, Sliv-er buck-les on his knee; He'll come back and marry me, Pret-ty Bob-by Shaf - to. Bob by Shaf-to's fat and fair, eyes of blue and yel-low hair; He's my love for - ev-er more, Pret-ty Bob-by Shaf - to.

Hot Cross Buns

Hot Cross Buns, nice fresh Hot Cross Buns, One a pen-ny Two a pen-ny Hot Cross Buns.

OLD KING COLE

Old King Cole was a happy carefree ruler and his kingdom was a land of sunshine and melody, for he was a lover of music. If there were troubles, he'd call for his number one court fiddler, and they would play and talk and play and talk. And before you knew it, the trouble would just dance right out of the castle window. And sometimes he'd call for his court fiddler number two, and sometimes for his number three, and they would fiddle and the castle would ring with melody. Everybody would forget his troubles and the King would set a large feast and proclaim a royal holiday. He'd call for his bowl and have it brought to him filled to the top with gold, and everyone would be given a share. While he sat on his big throne and smoked his pipe, he'd call for his three fiddlers to play for his merry people so they could all dance and sing. What a merry old soul he was!

Old King Cole

Old King Cole was a mer-ry old soul, yes a mer-ry old soul was he; He

call'd for his pipe, and he call'd for his bowl, And he call'd for his fid-dlers three.

Georgie Porgie

Geor-gie Por-gie, pud-ding and pie, Kiss'd the girls and made them cry;

When the girls came out to play, Geor-gie Por-gie ran a-way.

Simple Simon

Sim - ple Si - mon   met   a   pie man   Go - ing   to   the   fair;   Said
Said   the man   to   Sim - ple Si - mon   Show me first your   penny,   Said

Sim - ple Si - mon   to   the   pie man,   "Let   me   taste your   ware."
Sim - ple Si - mon   to   the   pie man,   "'Deed   I   have not   any."

Pussy-Cat, Pussy Cat

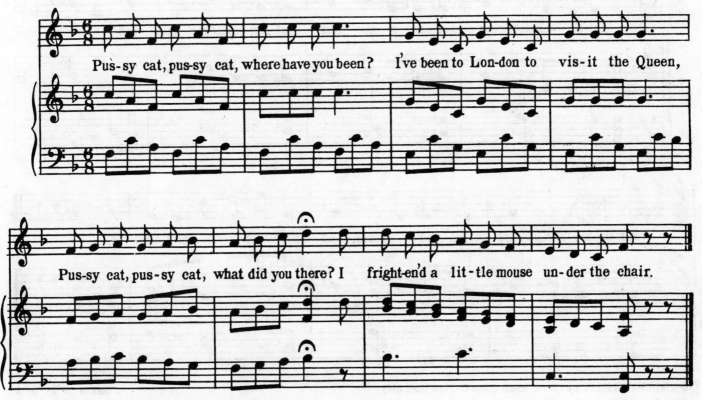

Pus - sy cat, pus - sy cat, where have you been?   I've been to Lon-don to   vis - it the Queen,

Pus - sy cat, pus - sy cat, what did you there? I   fright-en'd a   lit - tle mouse un - der the chair.

     Made in U.S.A.

Little Boy Blue

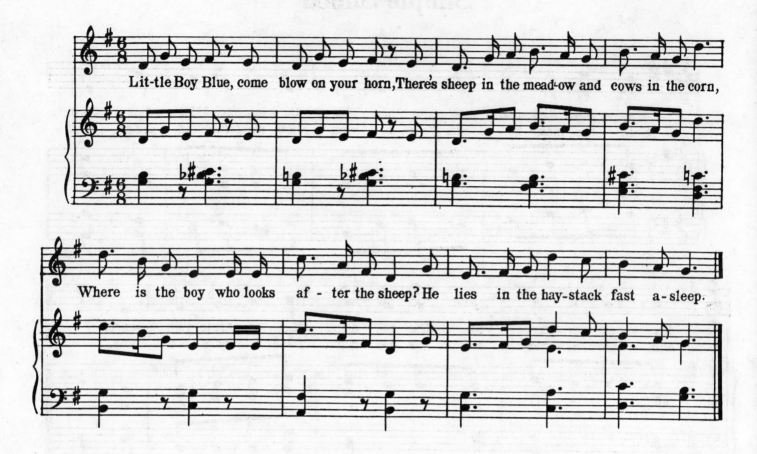

Lit-tle Boy Blue, come blow on your horn, There's sheep in the mead-ow and cows in the corn,

Where is the boy who looks af-ter the sheep? He lies in the hay-stack fast a-sleep.

Little Jack Horner

Lit-tle Jack Hor-ner sat in a cor-ner Eat-ing his Christ-mas pie, He

stuck in his thumb, And pulled out a plum, And said "What a good boy am I."

Made in U. S. A.

Lucy Locket

Lu - cy Lock - et lost her pock - et, Kit - ty Fish - er found it, but not a pen - ny was in it, Ex - cept a rib - bon round it.

Mary Had A Little Lamb

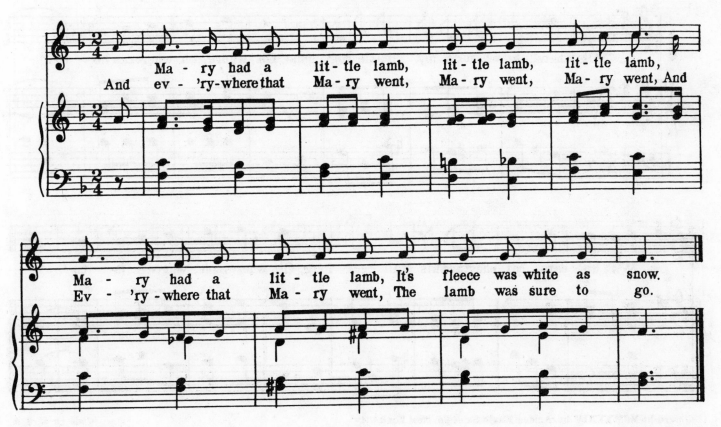

And ev - 'ry-where that Ma - ry went, Ma - ry went, Ma - ry went, And
Ma - ry had a lit - tle lamb, lit - tle lamb, lit - tle lamb,

Ma - ry had a lit - tle lamb, It's fleece was white as snow.
Ev - 'ry-where that Ma - ry went, The lamb was sure to go.

Made in U.S.A.

Jack Spratt

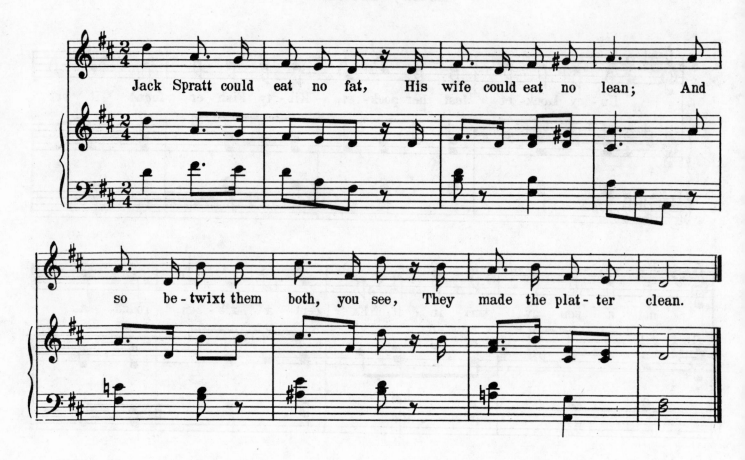

Jack Spratt could eat no fat, His wife could eat no lean; And so be-twixt them both, you see, They made the plat-ter clean.

Where Has My Little Dog Gone?

Oh where, oh where is my lit-tle dog gone, Oh where, oh where can he be? With his ears cut short and his tail cut long, Oh where, oh where is he?

Made in U. S. A.

See Saw, Margery Daw

Ride A Cock Horse To Banbury Cross

Three Blind Mice

Three blind mice, Three blind mice See how they run!

See how they run, They all run aft-er the farm-er's wife; Who cut off their tails with a

carv-ing knife; Did you ev-er see such a sight in your life as three blind mice.

Fiddle-De-Dee

Fid-dle de dee, Fid-dle de dee, The fly has mar-ried the bum-ble bee.
Fid-dle de dee, Fid-dle de dee, The fly has mar-ried the bum-ble bee.

Made in U.S.A.

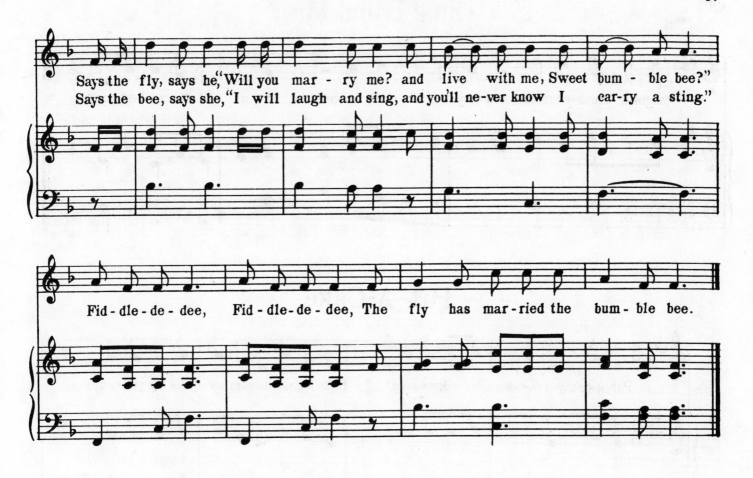

Says the fly, says he, "Will you mar - ry me? and live with me, Sweet bum - ble bee?"
Says the bee, says she, "I will laugh and sing, and you'll ne-ver know I car-ry a sting."

Fid - dle - de - dee, Fid - dle - de - dee, The fly has mar - ried the bum - ble bee.

There Was A Crooked Man

There was a crook-ed man, and he ran a crook-ed mile He

found a crook-ed six pence up - on a crook-ed stile: He bought a crook-ed cat, Which

Made in U. S. A.

caught a crook-ed mouse, And they all liv'd to-geth-er in a lit-tle crook-ed house.

Pat-A-Cake

Pat-a-cake, pat-a-cake, ba - ker's man! Bake a cake mas-ter as quick as you can,

Prick it, and nick it and mash it with T, And there will be plen-ty for ba-by and me, for

ba - by and me, for ba - by and me, And there will be plen-ty for ba - by and me.

The Fairy Ship

I saw a ship a-sail - ing, A sail - ing on the sea, And
The four and twen-ty sail - ors, That stood be-tween the decks, Were

it was deep - ly la - den With pret - ty things for me, There were
four and twen - ty white mice, With rings a - bout their necks, The

cook - ies in the cab - in sweets and al-monds in the hold; The
cap - tain was a snow white duck, With jew - els on his back; And

sails were made of sil - ver silk, And the mask was sol - id gold.
when this fai - ry ship set sail, The cap - tain, he said "Quack."

   Made in U.S.A.

HEY DIDDLE DIDDLE

Tabby, the pussy cat, had just finished drinking the milk that old Bossy, the cow, had given her, and she thought to herself as she sat purring a happy little song—"I wonder is there some way I can repay old Bossy for her kindness." At last she spoke.

"Meow, Mrs. Cow, would you like to dance?"

"Moo," said the cow, "but we have no music and who can dance without music."

Just then Prince, the little dog who had been listening, spoke up.

"Woof, woof," he said, "up on the table over there is the master's music maker and the stick he uses."

"Moo," said the cow, "do not touch that, the master loves it. That is his fiddle and the stick is his bow."

"Meow, meow, I shall make music to dance," said the cat, as she climbed up on the table and carefully lifted the fiddle and bow, as she had seen her master do.

"Meow, meow, get ready to dance," she said, and drew the bow over the strings, and out came a terrible noise.

Hey, Diddle, Diddle

Hey, did-dle, did-dle, The cat and the fid-dle, The cow jump'd o-ver the moon; The lit-tle dog laughed to see such sport, And the dish ran a-way with the spoon:

Humpty Dumpty

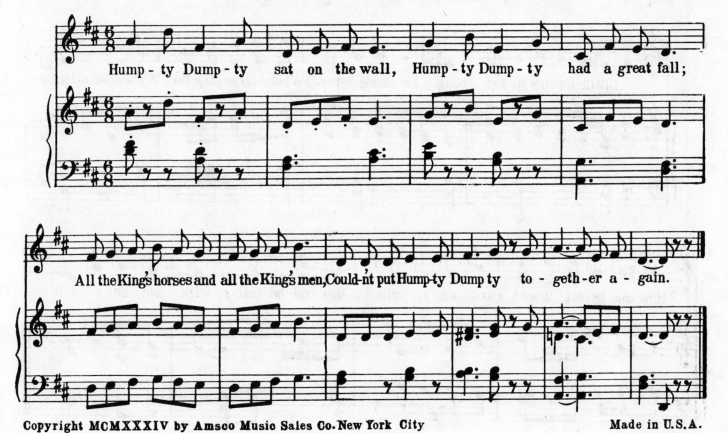

Hump-ty Dump-ty sat on the wall, Hump-ty Dump-ty had a great fall; All the King's horses and all the King's men, Could-n't put Hump-ty Dump ty to-geth-er a-gain.

Copyright MCMXXXIV by Amsco Music Sales Co. New York City

Little Miss Muffitt

Lit tle Miss Muf - fitt sat on a tuf - fet, Eat - ing some curds and whey, There came a big spid - er, And sat down be side her, And fright-end Miss Muf-fet a - way.

Little Tommy Tucker

Lit-tle Tom-my Tuck-er Sing for your sup-per, What shall he sing for White bread and but-ter. How can he cut it with - out an -y knife? How can he mar-ry with - out an -y wife?

Made in U.S.A.

Baby Bunting

Bye, Bye, Ba - by Bunt - ing, Dad - dy's gone a - hunt - ing To

fetch a lit - tle rab - bit skin, To wrap his Ba - by Bunt - ing in,

If All The World Were Paper

If all the world were pa - per, And all the sea were ink, And

all the trees were bread and cheese, What would we ev - er drink?

Made in U.S.A.

Cherries Ripe

The Little Woman

There was a lit-tle wo-man, as I've been told, Oh, me,
did-dle, did-dle, dee, Who was not ver-y young, nor not ver-y old,
Oh, me, did-dle, did-dle, dee, She went to mar-ket
on a mar-ket day, And she fell a-sleep up-on the King's High-way.
Fol de rol de lol, lol, lol, lol, lol, Dee, Dee, did-dle did-dle dee.

Made in U.S.A.

DICKORY DICKORY DOCK

The big clock in the hall had just struck twelve o'clock and was chuckling to himself, happy in the thought that another day's work was finished, when he happened to look down at his feet to see where that funny pitter patter noise came from. And he almost dropped his hands for a second from fright. For there, right in front of him on the floor, stood two little mice, talking.

"Squeak, squeak," said one to the other, "This is the bad clock that keeps us awake and frightened with its tick, tock, tick, tock, and bong, bong, when it sings all through the night."

"Squeak, squeak," said the other mouse, "What can we do? It is so big and has such funny hands and face that I'm afraid even to look at it."

"Squeak, squeak," said the other little mouse, "It has just made its biggest noise and it must be tired, so I will climb up inside and see if I can stop it."

So he went around and around the big clock. but he could not find a hole, so he gnawed and gnawed, while high above him the big clock went tick, tock, tick, tock, as it kept on with its work of telling time. At last the mouse gnawed a hole just big enough to squeeze through.

"Squeak, squeak," he called to the other mouse, "You stand there and watch for the black cat and I will climb up in the clock."

All this had taken a much longer time than he thought. He climbed up and up, way up to the top, and just then the clock went - - - Bong!

Dickory, Dickory, Dock

Dick-o-ry, dick-o-ry dock; The mouse ran up the clock; The clock struck one; The mouse ran down, Dick-o-ry, dick-o-ry dock.

Goosey Goosey Gander

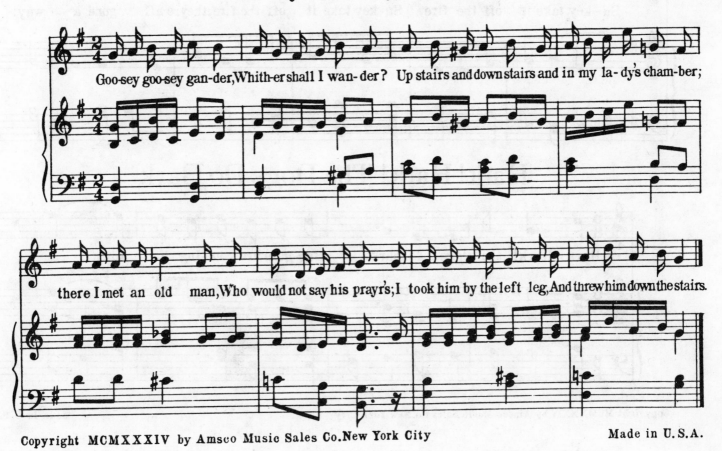

Goo-sey goo-sey gan-der, Whith-er shall I wan-der? Up stairs and down stairs and in my la-dy's cham-ber; there I met an old man, Who would not say his prayr's; I took him by the left leg, And threw him down the stairs.

Polly, Put The Kettle On

Hark! Hark! The Dogs Do Bark

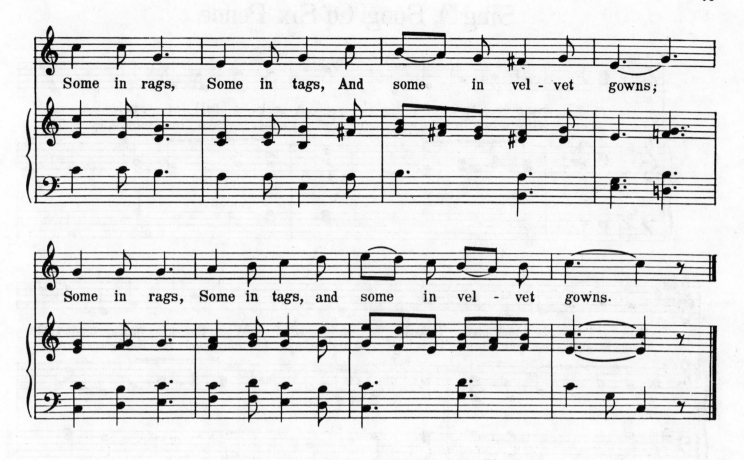

Some in rags, Some in tags, And some in vel - vet gowns;

Some in rags, Some in tags, and some in vel - vet gowns.

To Market, To Market

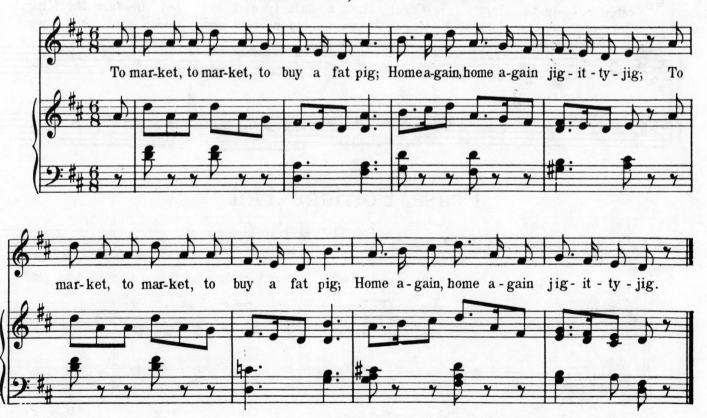

To mar-ket, to mar-ket, to buy a fat pig; Home a-gain, home a-gain jig - it - ty - jig; To

mar-ket, to mar-ket, to buy a fat pig; Home a-gain, home a-gain jig - it - ty - jig.

Sing A Song Of Six Pence

Sing a song of six - pence, A pock - et full of rye,
The King was in the count - ing house, Count - ing out his mon - ey The

Four and twen-ty black birds Baked in a pie; When the pie was open pen'd, The
queen was in the par - lor eat-ing bread and hon-ey, The maid was in the gar - den

birds be-gan to sing, Wasn't that a dain-ty dish to set be-fore the King.
Hang-ing out the clothes A - long came a black- bird and peck'd off her nose.

Pease Porridge Hot

Pease porridge hot, pease porridge cold, pease porridge in the pot nine days old.

Made in U. S.A

There Was An Old Woman

There was an old wo-man who lived in a shoe; She had
so man-y chil-dren, She did-n't know what to do: She gave them some broth with-
out an-y bread; She whipped them all sound-ly and put them to bed.

Taffy Was A Welshman

Taf-fy was a Welsh-man,Taf-fy was a thief, Taf-fy came to my house,and stole a piece of beef,
Then I went to his house, Taf-fy was not home, I went to Taffy's house,and stole a mar-row bone.

Made in U. S. A.

JACK and JILL

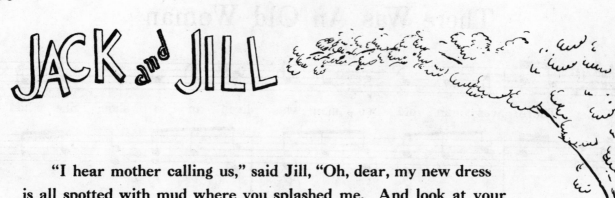

"I hear mother calling us," said Jill, "Oh, dear, my new dress is all spotted with mud where you splashed me. And look at your shoes—wet right through, Jack. But maybe mother won't notice it. You run ahead, Jack, and see what mother wants us for."

"It's almost supper time," said their mother, "and not a drop of water in the house. Take a pail and go up the hill to the spring and bring back some water. Be careful, Jack, the hill is steep, so don't play on the way. You might fall all the way down. Take Jill along so she can help you carry the pail."

So they remembered their mother's warning, at least until they had climbed the hill and filled the pail from the cool spring.

"Let's make believe the pail is filled with gold," said Jill, "and giants are chasing us." So they swung the pail back and forth and ran a little bit, when all of a sudden Jack tripped and Jill let go of the pail and he tumbled and rolled down the hill with the pail tumbling after him. Jill, frightened, tried to run and catch him and she tumbled bumpty bump all the way down after him, till she came to a stop right next to where Jack lay crying.

"Oh, look, there's a big lump on your head, and I'm all full of scratches, but don't cry—I'll go fill the pail and put some cold water on the bump. And after this, we'll listen to mother and always do as she says."

Jack And Jill

Jack and Jill went up the hill, To fetch a pail of wa - ter;

Jack fell down, And broke his crown, And Jill came tum - bling af - ter.

Little Bo-Peep

Lit-tle Bo-Peep has lost her sheep, And don't know where to find them,

Leave them a-lone, and they'll come home, Wag-ging their tails be-hind them.

Made in U. S. A.

Ding, Dong, Bell

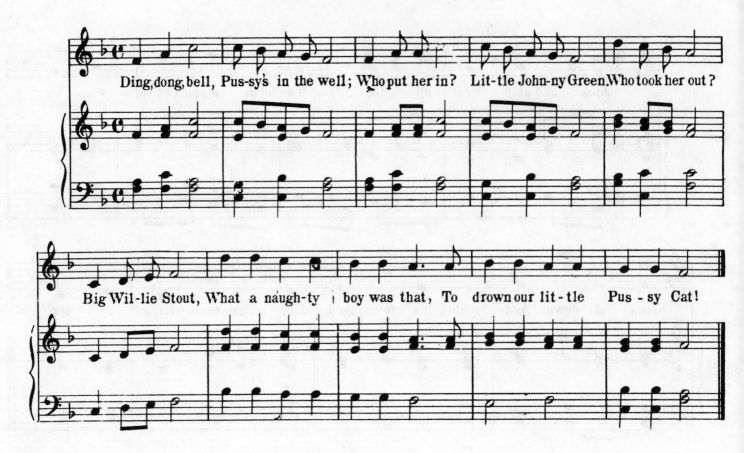

Ding, dong, bell, Pus-sy's in the well; Who put her in? Lit-tle John-ny Green. Who took her out?

Big Wil-lie Stout, What a naugh-ty boy was that, To drown our lit-tle Pus-sy Cat!

O Pretty Polly

Oh pret-ty Pol-ly, don't you cry, You'll be hap-py by and by,

When he comes he'll dress in blue, That's a sign he'll mar-ry you.

Made in U.S.A.

Pop! Goes The Weasel

All a-round the cob - bler's bench The mon-key chased the wea - sel; The

mon - key tho't 'twas all in fun, Pop! goes the wea - sel!

I've no time to wait or sigh, No pa-tience to wait 'till by and by;

Kiss me quick, I'm off, good bye, Pop! goes the wea - sel.

Made in U.S.A.

The Lost Doll

Oh, Dear! What Can The Matter Be?

Oh, dear! What can the mat-ter be? Dear, dear, what can the mat-ter be? Oh, dear!
What can the mat-ter be? John-ny's so long at the fair. He prom-ised to buy me a
trin-ket to please me, And then for a smile, Oh he vowed he would tease me, He
prom-ised to bring me a bunch of blue rib-bons, To tie up my bon-nie brown hair.

Oh, dear! What can the mat-ter be? Dear, dear, what can the mat-ter be? Oh, dear!
What can the mat-ter be? John-ny's so long at the fair. He prom-ised to bring me a
bas-ket of pos-ies, A gar-land of lil-ies, A gift of red ros-es, A
lit-tle straw hat to set off the blue rib-bons, That tie up my bon-nie brown hair.

Made in U. S. A.

Lullaby
(Erminie)

E. Jakobowski

Dear moth-er in dreams I see her, With loved face sweet and calm, And hear her voice with love re-joice When nest-ling on her arm. I think how she soft-ly press'd me, Of the tears in each glist-'ning eye_____, As her watch she'd keep, When she rock'd to sleep, Her

Made in U. S. A.

Sweet Dreamland Faces

W. M. Hutchinson

Bring - ing sweet mem - 'ries, ___ Of the long a - go.

Let Us Sing Merrily

Let us sing mer - ri - ly, Light - ly and cheer - i - ly,

Let us be gay. Throw a - way sor - row, Why should we

bor - row Tears from to - mor - row, To dark - en our day.

 Made in U. S. A.

The May Queen

Alfred Tennyson

Wm R. Dempster

You must wake and call me ear - ly, caH me ear - ly moth-er dear; To

mor-row will be the hap-pi-est time of all the glad new year; Of

all the glad new year, moth-er, the mad-dest, mer-ri-est day: For

I'm to be Queen o' the May; moth-er I'm to be Queen o' the May. I

Made in U.S.A.

sleep so sound all night moth-er, that I shall nev-er a - wake,—— If you

do not call me loud when the day be-gins to break: But

I must gath - er knots of flow'rs, and buds and gar-lands gay, For

I'm to be Queen o' the May, moth-er, I'm to be Queen o' the May.

I Am Happy Mother Darling

Mrs. M. A. Kidder

Geo. W. Persley

I am hap - py, moth-er dar - ling, With your kiss up - on my
I am hap - py, fa - ther dear - est, With your bless - ing and your
I have said my pray'r, dear moth - er, "Now I lay me down to

brow, With my hand clasped in your dear one, I can sleep, Oh! sweet-ly
kiss, With the sweet "good-night" you gave me, Which I hope to nev - er
sleep," And my Fa - ther up in heav - en, He my in - fant soul will

now I can sleep and dream of an - gels, With their gar - ments soft and
miss. I am hap - py, broth-er, sis - ter, Though the sun has gone to
keep. Now I'll close my eyes in slum - ber Till the ro - sy morn - ing

white, Hov-'ring 'round a-bout my pil - low, Guard-ing me till morn-ing
rest, For the stars are soft-ly shin - ing, And your lit - tle one is
light, I am hap - py, moth-er dar - ling, Now a fond, a last good-

Made in U.S.A.

light. I am hap-py moth-er dar-ling, With your kiss up-on my
blest.
night.

brow, With my hand clasped in your dear one I can sleep, oh! sweet-ly now.

Dolly And Her Mamma

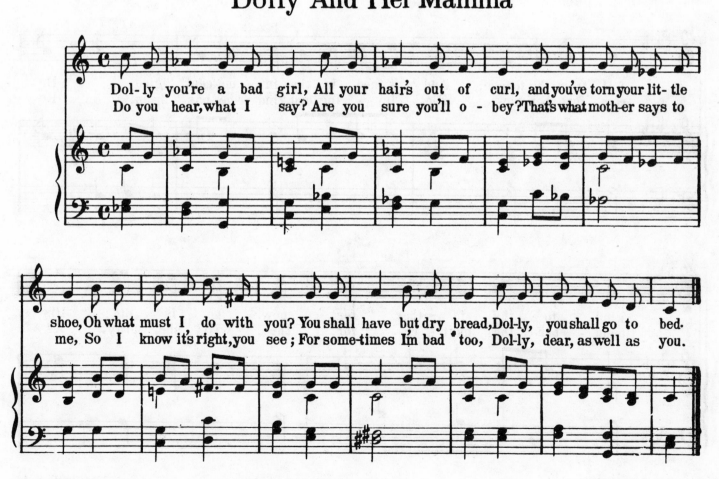

Dol-ly you're a bad girl, All your hair's out of curl, and you've torn your lit-tle
Do you hear, what I say? Are you sure you'll o - bey? That's what moth-er says to

shoe, Oh what must I do with you? You shall have but dry bread, Dol-ly, you shall go to bed.
me, So I know it's right, you see; For some-times I'm bad too, Dol-ly, dear, as well as you.

Be Kind To The Loved Ones At Home

Be kind to thy fa-ther, for when thou wert young, Who
Be kind to thy moth-er, for lo! on her brow May

loved thee so fond-ly as he? He caught the first ac-cent that
trac-es of sor-row be seen; Oh! well may thou cher-ish and

fell from thy tongue, And joined in thy in-no-cent glee. Be-
com-fort her now, For lov-ing and kind she has been. Re-

kind to thy fa-ther for now he is old; His
mem-ber thy moth-er for thee will she pray, As

locks in-ter-ming-led with gray; His foot-steps are fee-ble, once
long as God giv-eth her breath; With ac-cents of kind-ness then

fear-less and bold; Thy fa-ther is pass-ing a-way.
cheer her lone way, E'en to the dark val-ley death.

The Fairy Ring

Let us laugh, and let us sing, Danc-ing in a mer-ry ring;
Like the sea-sons of the year, 'Round the cir-cle glad-ly here;

We'll be fair-ies on the green; Sport-ing 'round the fai-ry queen.
I'll be Sum-mer, you'll be Spring; Danc-ing 'round the fai-ry ring.

Made in U.S.A.

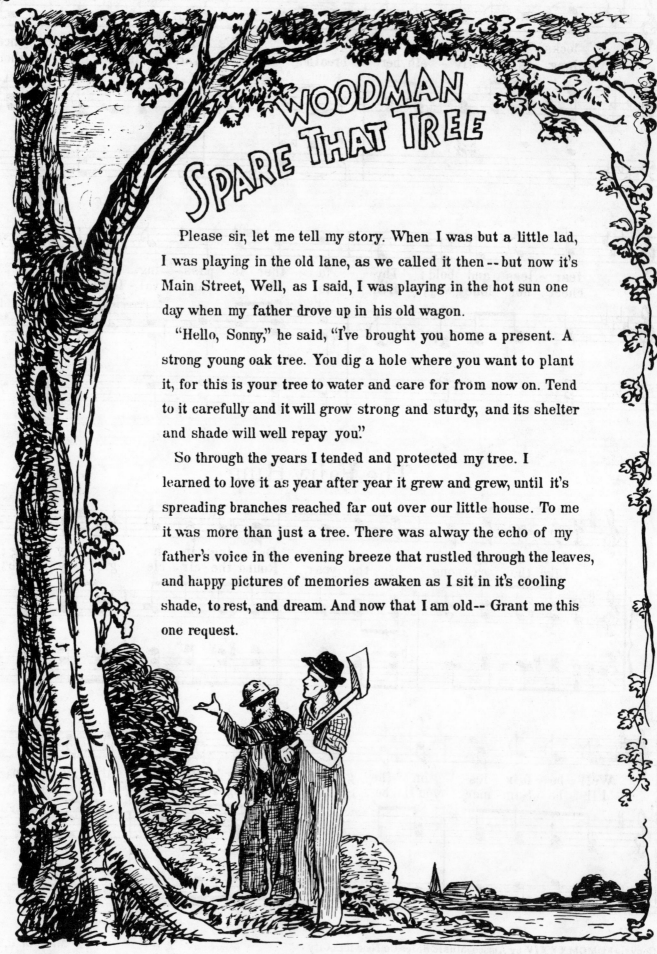

WOODMAN SPARE THAT TREE

Please sir, let me tell my story. When I was but a little lad, I was playing in the old lane, as we called it then -- but now it's Main Street, Well, as I said, I was playing in the hot sun one day when my father drove up in his old wagon.

"Hello, Sonny," he said, "I've brought you home a present. A strong young oak tree. You dig a hole where you want to plant it, for this is your tree to water and care for from now on. Tend to it carefully and it will grow strong and sturdy, and its shelter and shade will well repay you."

So through the years I tended and protected my tree. I learned to love it as year after year it grew and grew, until it's spreading branches reached far out over our little house. To me it was more than just a tree. There was alway the echo of my father's voice in the evening breeze that rustled through the leaves, and happy pictures of memories awaken as I sit in it's cooling shade, to rest, and dream. And now that I am old-- Grant me this one request.

Woodman, Spare That Tree

Henry Russell

Slowly *with feeling*

Wood - man spare that tree!___ Touch not a sin - gle
That old fa - mil - iar tree!___ Whose glo - ry and re -
When but an i - dle boy,___ I sought its grate - ful

bough; In youth it shel - ter'd me,___ And
nown; Are spread o'er land and sea,___ And
shade; In all their gush - ing joy,___ Here

I'll pro - tect it now. 'Twas my fore - fa - ther's
wouldst thou hack it down? Wood - man, for - bear thy_
too, my sis - ters play'd: My moth - er kiss'd me_

hand___ That placed it near his cot, There
stroke!___ Cut not it's earth - bound ties, Oh,
here;___ My fa - ther press'd my hand, For -

Made in U. S. A.

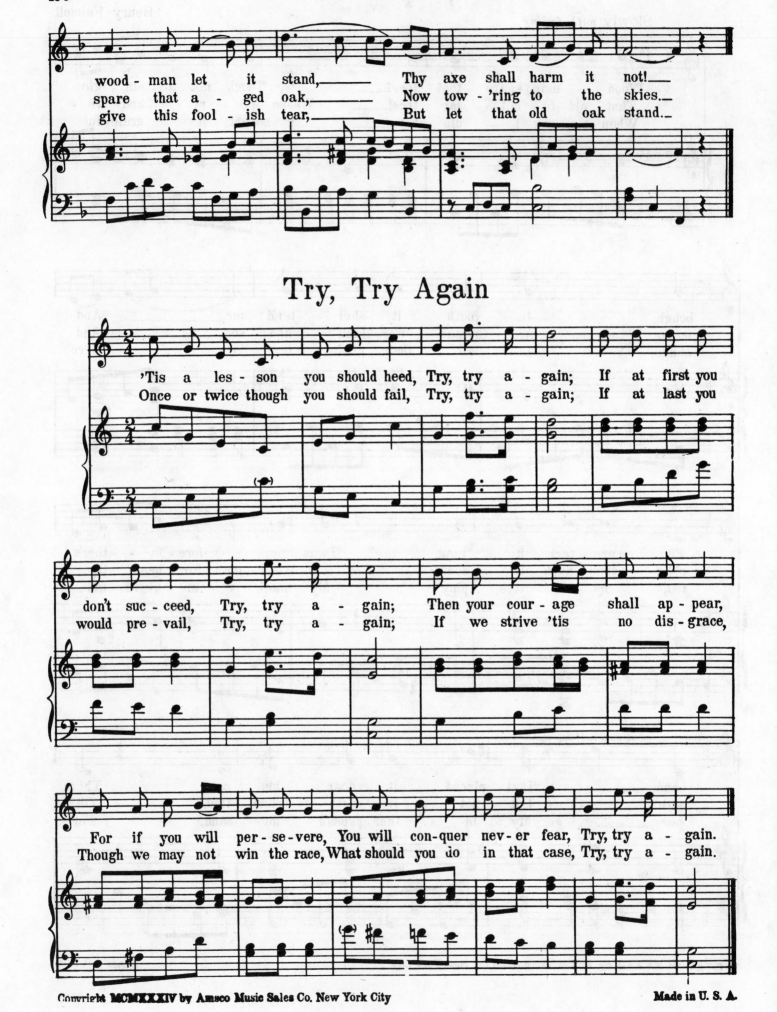

Try, Try Again

'Tis a les-son you should heed, Try, try a-gain; If at first you
Once or twice though you should fail, Try, try a-gain; If at last you

don't suc-ceed, Try, try a-gain; Then your cour-age shall ap-pear,
would pre-vail, Try, try a-gain; If we strive 'tis no dis-grace,

For if you will per-se-vere, You will con-quer nev-er fear, Try, try a-gain.
Though we may not win the race, What should you do in that case, Try, try a-gain.

The Jolly Miller

There was a jol-ly mil-ler once lived on the riv-er Dee,___ He
I live by the mill, she is to me like pa-rent, child, and wife!___ I

worked and sang from morn 'till night, No lark more blithe than he,___ And
would not change my sta - tion for an-y oth-er life,___ No

this the bur-den of his song for-ev-er used to be,___ "I
law- yer, sur-geon, doc-tor ev-er had a groan from me,___ I

care for no-bod-y, no, not I, And no-bod-y cares for me."___

Made in U.S.A.

Sailing

Godfrey Marks

Spirited

Sail - ing, sail - ing, O - ver the bound - ing main,___ For

man - y a storm - y wind shall blow, Er'e Jack comes home a - gain

Sail - ing, sail - ing, O - ver the bound - ing main,___ For

man - y a storm - y wind shall blow, Er'e Jack comes home a - gain.___

Made in U.S.A.

A FISH STORY

Raka Waga

King Arthur

When good King Ar-thur ruled this land, He was a wise old king, He
stole two pecks of bar-ley meal, To make a hot pud-ding.

Where Are You Going, My Pretty Maid?

Where are you go-ing to, my pret-ty maid? Where are you go-ing to, my pret-ty maid? I'm
Shall I go with you my pret ty maid? Shall I go with you my pret-ty maid?

go-ing a - milk - ing, "Sir," she said "I'm go-ing a - milk-ing Sir" she said.
"Yes, if you please, kind Sir," she said "Yes, if you please, kind Sir" she said.

Made in U. S. A.

Buy A Broom

From Deutsch-land I come with my light wares all la - den, To the
To brush a - way in - sects that some-times an - noy you, You'll

land where the bless - ing of free - dom doth bloom; Then
find it quite hand - y to use night and day; And

lis - ten, fair la - dy, and young pret - ty maid - en, Oh,
what bet - ter ex - er - cise pray can em - ploy you, Than to

buy of the wand - 'ring Ba - va - rian a broom.
sweep all vex - a - tions in - tru - ders a - way?

Made in U. S. A.

GIDDY AP HOBBY HORSE

Raka Waga

Gid - dy ap, gid - dy ap hob - by horse

Fast as your legs will fly, Gid - dy ap, gid - dy ap

down the hall, Moth er is bak-ing a pie.

Let Us Dance, Let Us Play

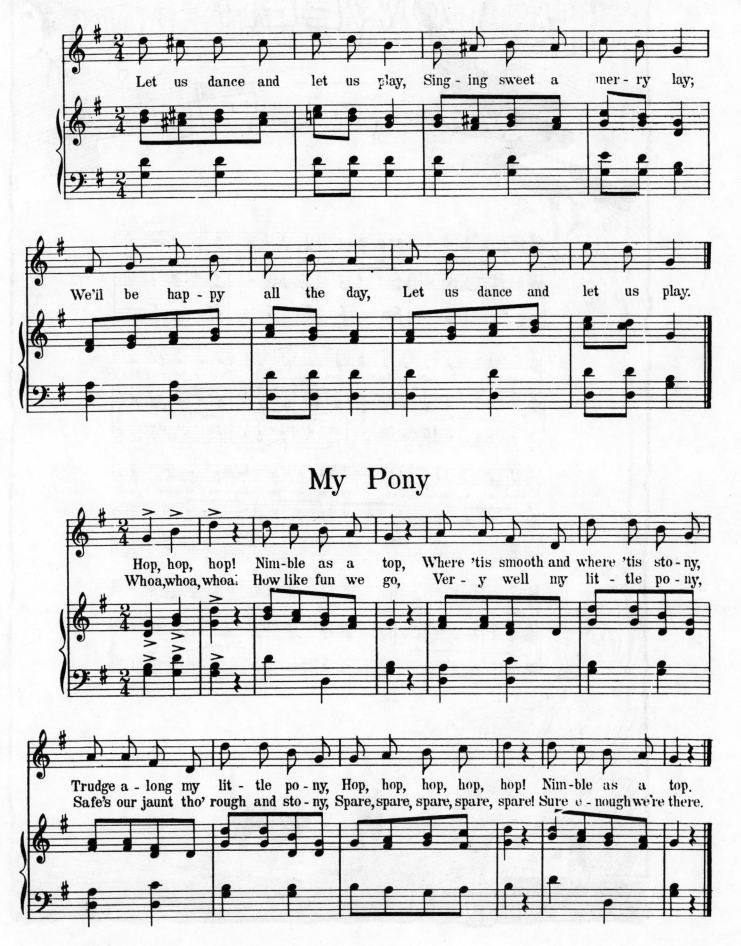

Let us dance and let us play, Sing-ing sweet a mer-ry lay;

We'll be hap-py all the day, Let us dance and let us play.

My Pony

Hop, hop, hop! Nim-ble as a top, Where 'tis smooth and where 'tis sto-ny,
Whoa, whoa, whoa! How like fun we go, Ver-y well my lit-tle po-ny,

Trudge a-long my lit-tle po-ny, Hop, hop, hop, hop, hop! Nim-ble as a top.
Safe's our jaunt tho' rough and sto-ny, Spare, spare, spare, spare, spare! Sure e-nough we're there.

HALLOWEEN

Raka Waga

Gob-lins and witch-es ride on a broom, Ghost-ly sha-dows steal 'round the room, to-night, To-night is Hal-low-e'en _____ Light up the pump-kins, dress in a sheet, Scare ev-'ry-bo-dy you hap-pen to meet to-night, To-night is Hal-low-e'en. _____

Deck The Hall

Hark! The Herald Angels Sing

Joyfully

F. Mendelssohn

Hark, the her-ald an-gels sing "Glo-ry to the new-born King!
Christ by high-est Heav'n a-dored; Christ the ev-er-last-ing Lord;
Hail! the Heav'n born Prince of peace! Hail! the Son of Right-eous-ness;

Peace on earth and mer-cy mild, God and sin-ners re-con-ciled."
Late in time be-hold him come, Off-spring of the fav-ored one.
Light and life to all he brings, Ris'n with heal-ing in his wings.

Joy-ful, all ye na-tions rise Join the tri-umph of the skies,
Veil'd in flesh, the God-head see; Hail th'in-car-nate De-i-ty:
Mild he lays his glo-ry by, Born that man no more can die.

With th'an-gel-ic host pro-claim, Christ is born in Beth-le-hem."
Pleased, as man, with men to dwell, Je-sus our Im-man-u-el!
Born to raise the Sons of earth, Born to give them se-cond birth.

Made in U.S.A.

Hark! the her-ald an-gels sing "Glo-ry to the new-born King."

Holy Night! Peaceful Night!

Franz Gruber

Slowly

Ho - ly night! peace-ful night! Thro' the dark-ness beams a light,
Si - lent night! ho-li-est night! Dark-ness flies and all is light!
Si - lent night! ho-li-est night! Guid-ing Star, O lend thy light!

Yon-der where they sweet vig - ils keep, O'er the Babe who in si - lent sleep,
Shep-herds hear the an - gels sing: Hal-le-lu - jah! hail the King!
See the East - ern wise men bring Gifts and hom-age to our King!

Rests in heav - en - ly peace, Rests in heav - en - ly peace.
Je - sus the Sav - iour is here! Je - sus the Sav - iour is here!
Je - sus the Sav - iour is here! Je - sus the Sav - iour is here!

Made in U. S. A.

A Carriage For Riding
(Dear Santa)

Carl Reinecke

A car - riage for rid - ing, A horse for be - strid - ing, A

jar full of ho - ney, A box for my mo - ney, A doll's house and

kit - chen, What things we'll be rich in! A book, too, to read, What

else can we need? Oh a flute and a fid - dle, Hey did - dle

The Christmas Tree
(Der Tannenbaum)

German Folk Song

Joyfully

O Christ-mas tree, O Christ-mas tree, how faith-ful are thy leaves; You
O Christ-mas tree, O Christ-mas tree, thy leaves teach me a les-son; For

bloom with sum-mer's fair-est rose, And in the win-ter's bit-ter snows; O
they give hope and con-stan-cy, Give strenth and cour-age un-to me; O

Christ-mas tree, O Christ-mas tree, how faith-ful are thy leaves!
Christ-mas tree, O Christ-mas tree, thy leaves teach me a les-son!

Song Of The New Year

A. H. Baldwin

Stephen Glover

Ring out, O bells, ring sil - ver sweet_ o'er

hill and moor and dell!_ In mel - low ech - oes,

let your chimes their hope - ful sto - ry tell._ Ring

out, ring out, all ju - bi - lant,_ this joy - ous glad_ re -

Made in U. S. A.

THE MULBERRY BUSH

Here we go 'round the mul-ber-ry bush, the mul-ber-ry bush, the mul-ber-ry bush,
This is the way we wash our clothes, we wash our clothes, we wash our clothes,

Here we go 'round the mul-ber-ry bush, so ear-ly in the morn-ing.
This is the way we wash our clothes, so ear-ly Mon-day morn-ing.

3. This is the way we iron our clothes, etc.
   So early Tuesday morning.

4. This is the way we scrub the floor, etc.
   So early Wednesday morning.

5. This is the way we mend our clothes, etc.
   So early Thursday morning.

6. This is the way we sweep the house, etc.
   So early Friday morning.

7. This is the way we bake our bread, etc.
   So early Saturday morning.

8. This is the way we go to church, etc.
   So early Sunday morning.

The game consists in suiting the actions to the words of each verse of the song. It is especially attractive for little girls.

Ring A Round A Rosy

All the children take hands, and dance around in a ring, and fall down at the last words

Ring a-round a ro-sy, pick a pret-ty po-sy,

All the girls in our town vote for Un-cle Jo-sy.

London Bridge

Lon-don bridge is fall-ing down, fall-ing down, fall-ing down,
Build it up with i-ron bars, i-ron bars, i-ron bars,

Lon-don bridge is fall-ing down, My fair la-dy.
Build it up with i-ron bars, My fair la-dy.

Two children form an arch by raising their arms above their heads to make a bridge for the other children to pass under— These two children secretly decide which one represents silver and which one gold. The other children now pass under the bridge formed by their arms. At the word "My fair lady," the bridge falls— the child who is caught is asked which he prefers—"gold or silver"— This child then takes its place behind the one who represents their choice and the game continues until all have been chosen. When all the children have been caught under the bridge, a tug of war between gold and silver ends the game.

Made in U.S.A

Musical Alphabet

Come, dear teach-er, hear me say What I can of A B C: A B C D
E F G, H I J K L M N O P; Q R S and T U V,
W (dou-ble you) and X Y Z Now you've heard my A B C, Tell me what you think of me.

The King Of France

The King of France with for-ty thous-and men, Rode up the hill and then rode down a-gain.
The King of France with for-ty thous-and men, Gave a sa-lute and then rode down a-gain.

Made in U. S. A.

Little Sally Waters

Lit - tle Sal - ly Wa - ters, sit - ting by the sun, Cry - ing and weep - ing for a nice young man. Rise Sal - ly rise, wipe off your eyes, Fly to the East, fly to the West, Fly to the one you love the best.

The children form a ring, with a child selected as "Sally Waters" in the center. Sally Waters sits on the ground, with her face in her hands as if weeping. The children dance around singing the verse, and as they sing "Rise Sally Rise" she rises and chooses a child from the ring to join her in the center. She then joins the ring, and the child takes her place. The game continues until each child has taken the part of "Sally" Waters."

Copyright MCMXXXIV by Amsco Music Sales Co. New York City

I'll Give You A Paper Of Pins

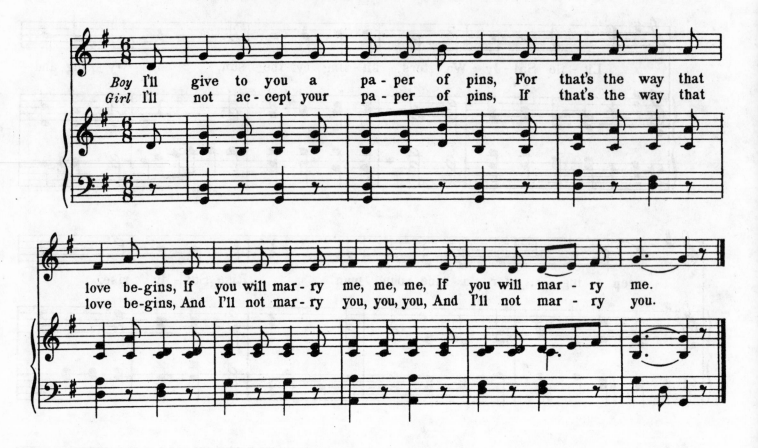

Boy I'll give to you a pa-per of pins, For that's the way that
Girl I'll not ac-cept your pa-per of pins, If that's the way that

love be-gins, If you will mar-ry me, me, me, If you will mar-ry me.
love be-gins, And I'll not mar-ry you, you, you, And I'll not mar-ry you.

Ten Little Indians

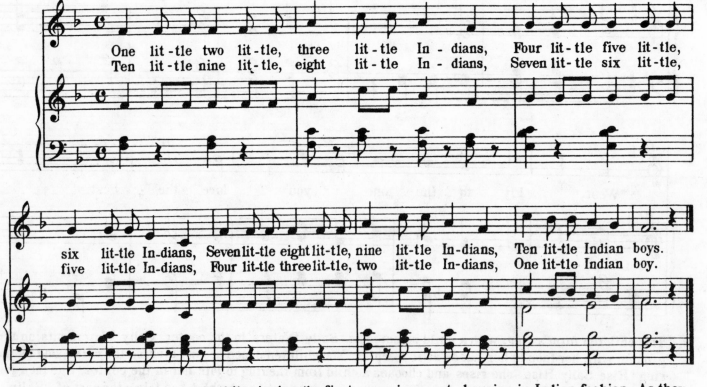

One lit-tle two lit-tle, three lit-tle In-dians, Four lit-tle five lit-tle,
Ten lit-tle nine lit-tle, eight lit-tle In-dians, Seven lit-tle six lit-tle,

six lit-tle In-dians, Seven lit-tle eight lit-tle, nine lit-tle In-dians, Ten lit-tle Indian boys.
five lit-tle In-dians, Four lit-tle three lit-tle, two lit-tle In-dians, One lit-tle Indian boy.

The children stand on line, and while singing the first verse jump out, hopping in Indian fashion. As they sing the second verse they hop back into line one by one in the same way.

Made in U.S.A.

The Farmer

The game consists of the children imitating the farmer's motions as he sows, reaps and threshes his wheat

Shall I show you how the farm-er Shall I show you how the farm-er Shall I
This is the way that the farm-er This is the way that the farm-er This is

show you how the farm-er sows his bar-ley and his wheat.
the way that the farm-er sows his bar-ley and his wheat.

Lazy Mary, Will You Get Up?

La-zy Ma-ry, will you get up, Will you get up, will you get up,
Oh no, moth-er, I won't get up, I won't get up, I won't get up,

La-zy Ma-ry, will you get up, Will you get up to-day. ___
Oh no, moth-er, I won't get up, I won't get up to-day. ___

A child selected to represent Lazy Mary, sits in the center of the ring as the children dance around her singing the first verse, Lazy Mary then sings the second verse – as she finishes – all the children try to get her up – and Lazy Mary tries to pull some other child down – any player falling is then chosen to play the part of Lazy Mary.

Hoddy Doddy,
With a round body,
Three feet and a wooden hat.
    What's that?
    (A Three-legged Iron Pot)

In marble walls as white as milk,
Lined with a skin as soft as silk;
Within a fountain crystal clear,
A golden apple doth appear.
No doors there are to this strong hold—
Yet thieves break in and steal the gold.
    (An Egg)

As high as a castle,
As weak as a wastle;
And all the king's horses
Cannot pull it down.
    (Smoke)

I'm in every one's way,
But no one I stop;
My four horns every day
In every way play,
And my head is nailed on at the top!
    (Turnstile)

A riddle, a riddle, as I suppose,
A hundred eyes, and never a nose.
    (A Potato)

There was a girl in our town,
Silk an' satin was her gown,
Silk an' satin, gold an' velvet,
Guess her name—three times I've tell'd it.
    (Ann)

Riddle me, riddle me, what is that
Over the head, and under the hat?
    (Hair)

Long legs, crooked thighs,
Little head and no eyes.
    (A pair of tongs.)

Black within, and red without;
Four corners round about.
    (A Chimney)

Riddle-me riddle me riddle-me-ree,
Perhaps you can tell what this riddle may be:
As deep as a house, as round as a cup,
And all the king's horses can't draw it up.
    (A Well)

Old Mother Twitchett had but one eye,
And a long tail, which she let fly;
And every time she went over a gap
She left a bit of her tail in a trap.
    (A Needle)

As soft as silk, as white as milk,
As bitter as gall, a strong wall,
And a green coat covers me all.
    (A Walnut)

Arthur O'Bower has broken his band,
He comes roaring up the land;
The King of Scots, with all his power
Cannot turn Arthur of the Bower.
    (The Wind)

Over the water,
And under the water,
And always with its head down.
    (A Ship's Nail)

Little Nanny Etticoat
In a white petticoat,
And a red nose;
The longer she stands
The shorter she grows.
    (A Candle)

Lives in winter,
Dies in summer,
And grows with its roots upward!
    (An Icicle)

A hill full, a hole full,
Yet you cannot catch a bowl full.
    (The Mist)

Itiskit, Itasket

I - tis - kit, I - tas - ket, A green and yel - low bas - ket, I

wrote a let - ter to my love, and on the way I lost it, I

lost, it, I lost it, And on the way I lost it.

When the words "I dropped it" are sung, a handerchief is dropped behind some child by another who runs around a circle of children playing. This child picks up the handerchief and as she runs around the circle of players, drops the handerchief behind some other child;--this continues until every child has had the handerchief.

Soldier Boy

One child is selected to represent a soldier— He marches past while the other children sing the verse as far as the words Red, White and Blue— The soldier then halts and sings the rest of verse— selecting another child to march with him— the game continues until all the children become soldiers.

Copyright MCMXXXIV by Amsco Music Sales Co. New York City

Oats, Peas, Beans And Barley Grow

The children form a circle around a child in the center representing a farmer. After the first four lines are sung they imitate the motion of a farmer, sowing, reaping, etc. They form in a ring again and the child representing a farmer selects a partner and both kneel during the second verse. The first child now chooses a child to take its place, and joins the ring.

Made in U. S. A.

Jenny Jones

One child represents Miss Jenny Jones and another child her mother. The players dance in a circle around them singing the verse "We've come to see Miss Jenny Jones" and the two children in the centre sing the answer "Miss Jenny Jones is a-washing" etc. When the mother says "Jenny is dead," the children run away in all directions. The first one caught takes her place in the centre of the circle and the game begins over again.

3. We've come to see,
   Miss Jenny is starching,

4. We've come to see,
   Miss Jenny is ironing,

5. We've come to see,
   Miss Jenny is sweeping,

6. We've come to see,
   Miss Jenny is sick a bed,

7. We've come to see,
   Miss Jenny is dying,

8. We've come to see,
   Miss Jenny is dead,

THE FARMER IN THE DELL

The farm-er in the dell, The farm-er in the dell,

Heigh ho the der-ry oh, The farm-er in the dell.

2. The farmer takes a wife, etc.

3. The wife takes the child, etc.

4. The child takes the nurse, etc.

5. The nurse takes the dog, etc.

6. The dog takes the cat, etc.

7. The cat takes the rat, etc.

8. The rat takes the cheese, etc.

9. The cheese stands alone, etc.

A child, representing the farmer stands in the center of a circle of children, and chooses another child, "the wife" at the end of the second verse; this one chooses another, "the child," and so on until "the cheese" is selected, after which the game begins over again.

Home, Sweet Home

Sir Henry Bishop

The Old Oaken Bucket

Samuel Woodworth

How dear to this heart are the scenes of my child-hood, When
The or-chard, the mead-ow, the deep tan-gled wild-wood, And
D.C. The old oak-en buck-et, the i-ron bound buck-et, The

fond rec-ol-lec-tion pre-sents them to view
ev-'ry loved spot which my in-fan-cy knew. The wide spread-ing pond and the
moss cov-ered buck-et that hung in the well. The cot of my fa-ther, the

mill that stood by it, The bridge and the rock where the cat-a-ract fell;
dai-ry-house nigh it, And e'en the rude buck-et that hung in the well.

II

The moss cover'd bucket I hail as a treasure,
For often at noon when return'd from the field,
I found it the source of an exquisite pleasure,
The purest and sweetest that nature can yield.
How ardent I seized it with hands that were glowing
And quick to the white pebbled bottom it fell.
Then soon with the emblem of truth over flowing,
And dripping with coolness it rose from the well.
The old oaken bucket, the iron-bound bucket,
The moss cover'd bucket that hung in the well.

III

How soon from the green mossy rim to receive it,
As pois'd on the curb it reclin'd to my lips,
Not a full flowing goblet could tempt me to leave it,
Tho' filled with the nectar that Jupiter sips.
And now far removed from the loved situation,
The tear of regret will intrusively swell.
As fancy reverts to my father's plantation,
And sighs for the bucket that hung in the well.
The old oaken bucket, the iron-bound bucket,
The moss cover'd bucket that hung in the well.

What Is Home Without A Mother?

Alice Hawthorne

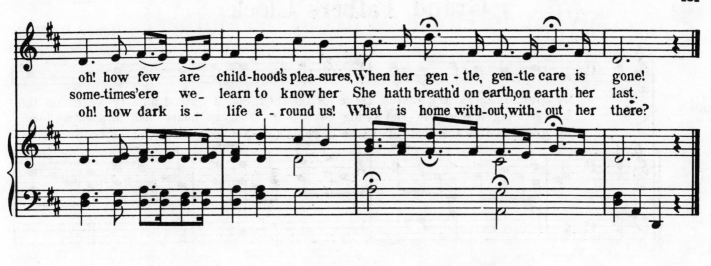

oh! how few are child-hood's plea-sures, When her gen - tle, gen-tle care is gone!
some-times'ere we_ learn to know her She hath breath'd on earth, on earth her last.
oh! how dark is _ life a - round us! What is home with-out, with - out her there?

The Dearest Spot On Earth

The dear - est spot on earth to me is home, sweet home; The
I've taught my heart the way to prize my home, sweet home; I've

Fine

fai - ry land I long to see is home, sweet home There how charm'd the sense of hear-ing,
learn'd to look with lov-er's eyes on home, sweet home There, where vows were tru - ly plight-ed,

Fine

D. C.

There, where love is so en-dear-ing! All the world is not so cheer-ing as home, sweet home
There, where hearts are so u - nit - ed! All the world be-side I've slight-ed for home, sweet home

D. C.

 Made in U. S. A.

Grand Father's Clock

Henry C. Work

stopp'd short nev-er to go a-gain When the old man

died. Nine-ty years, with-out slum-ber-ing (tick, tock, tick, tock,) His

life - se-conds num-ber-ing (tick, tock, tick, tock,) It stopp'd short

nev-er to go a-gain When the old man died._____

Love's Old Sweet Song

J. L. Molloy

Once in the dear dead days be-yond re-call, When on the world the
E - ven to-day we hear love's song of yore, Deep in our hearts it

mists be-gan to fall, Out of the dreams that rose in hap-py throng,
dwells for-ev-er more, Foot-steps may fal - ter, wear-y grow the way,

How in our hearts love sang an old sweet song, And in the dusk where
Still we can hear it at the close of day, So in the end when

fell the fire-light gleam, Soft-ly it wove it-self in-to our dream.
life's dim shad-ows fall, Love will be found the sweet-est song of all.

Just a song at twi - light, When the lights are low;

And the flick - 'ring shad - ows Soft - ly come and go;

Tho' the heart be wear-y, Sad the day and long, Still to us at

twi - light, Comes love's old song, Comes love's old sweet song.

America

Samuel F. Smith

Joyously

My coun-try, 'tis of thee, Sweet land of lib-er-ty
My na-tive coun-try thee, Land of the no-ble free,
Let mu-sic swell the breeze, And ring from all the trees,
Our fath-ers' God, to thee, Au-thor of lib-er-ty,

Of thee I sing; Land where my
Thy name I love; I love thy
Sweet free-dom's song; Let mor-tal
To thee we sing; Long may our

fath-ers died, Land of the Pil-grims' pride,
rocks and rills, Thy woods and tem-pled hills,
tongues a-wake, Let all that breathe par-take,
land be bright, With free-dom's ho-ly light,

From ev-'ry moun-tain side, Let free-dom ring.
My heart with rap-ture thrills, Like that a-bove.
Let rocks their si-lence break, The sound pro-long.
Pro-tect us by thy might, Great God, our King.

STAR SPANGLED BANNER

It was early in the afternoon of September 13, 1814, and Francis Scott Key, a young Baltimore lawyer, was working in his study. It had been a busy morning filled with excitement, for news had been received that the British Fleet was anchored off Baltimore.

There came a knock at the door. Wondering who it could be at this time of the day, he called "come in." A young lad entered.

"Sir," he said, "I have a message—Doctor Beanes, a brave and patriotic soldier from Upper Marlborough, Virginia, has been captured and is held a prisoner on one of the ships of the British fleet. We are seeking his release and ask your help."

"My lad," said Francis Scott Key, "this is sad news. I shall gather some fellow-men, and there is a boat I know of that we can use. We shall sail at once to the enemy's ships, under a flag of truce. Perhaps we can arrange for the Doctor's release.

And so the small party set sail for the British fleet, and Francis Scott Key was taken to the British Admiral who was polite and listened to his story. But when it was time to start to return, he would not let their boat leave, for the Admiral had planned to attack the city of Baltimore's principal defense, Fort McHenry, that very night, and he was afraid that his plans would become known if they allowed the boat to return. So Francis Scott Key was held on the ship, and as soon as it became dark, the British started to bombard Fort McHenry. All night long he watched the flashes of the guns—straining his eyes, peering through the darkness to catch a fleeting outline of the fort. Several times the firing stopped and he thought the fort had surrendered. But as the first rays of dawn crept out of the east, he saw the outlines of the fort and there above it, his country's flag was still waving. Inspired by the joyful sight, he took an envelope from his pocket and wrote . . . .

The Star Spangled Banner

Francis Scott Key

rock - ets red glare, the bombs burst - ing, in air, Gave
catch - es the gleam of the morn - ings first beam, In full
re - fuge could save the hire - ling and slave, From the
con - quer we must, for our cause it is just, And

proof thro' the night that our flag was still there.
glo - ry re - flect - ed now shines in the stream. Oh
ter - ror of flight or the gloom of the grave.
this be our mot - to, "In God is our trust!"

say, does that__ star span - gled ban - ner yet wave,__ O'er the

land ___ of the free, and the home of the brave!

Marching Through Georgia

     Made in U. S. A.

So we sang the chor-us from At - lan-ta to the sea, While we were march-ing thro' Geor - gia.

Yankee Doodle

Oh Yan-kee Doo-dle came to town, Up - on a lit-tle po - ny, He stuck a fea-ther

in his cap, And called it mac-a - ro - ni Yan-kee Doo-dle doo - dle do,

Yan-kee Doo-dle dan - dy; All the lads and las-sies are as sweet as sug-ar can-dy

Hail, Columbia

Hail Columbia, happy land, Hail, ye heroes,
Im - mor - tal pa - triots rise once more De - fend your rights, de -
Sound,_ sound the trump of fame, Let, Wash - ing -

Heav'n born band, Who fought and bled in Free - dom's_ cause, Who
fend your shores, Let no rude foe with im - pi - ous hand, Let
ton's great name, Ring thro' the world with loud_ ap_ plause, Ring

fought and bled in Free - dom's_ cause, And when the storm of
no rude foe with im - pi - ous hand, In - vade the shrine where
thro' the world with loud_ ap - plause, Let ev - 'ry clime to

war was gone, En - joyed_ the_ peace your val - or won, Let
sa - cred lies, Of toil_ and_ blood the well - earn'd prize, While
free - dom dear,_____ Lis - ten_ with a joy - ful ear, With

The Red, White And Blue

Oh, Co-lum-bia the gem of the o-cean, The home of the brave and the
When war wing'd its wide des-o - la-tion, And threat-ened the land to de-
The star-spangled ban-ner bring hith- er, O'er Co - lum-bia's true sons let it

free, ___ The shrine of each pa-triot's de - vo-tion, A
form, ___ The ark then of free-dom's foun - da-tion, Co -
wave, ___ May the wreaths they have worn nev - er with - er, Nor its

world of - fers hom - age to thee ___ Thy man-dates make he - roes as -
lum - bia rode safe thro' the storm ___ With the gar-lands of vic - t'ry a
stars cease to shine on the brave ___ May the ser - vice u - ni - ted ne'er

sem - ble, ___ When Lib - er - ty's form stands in view, ___ Thy
round her, ___ When so proud - ly she bore her brave crew, ___ With her
sev - er, ___ But hold to their col - ors so true, ___ The

Made in U.S.A.

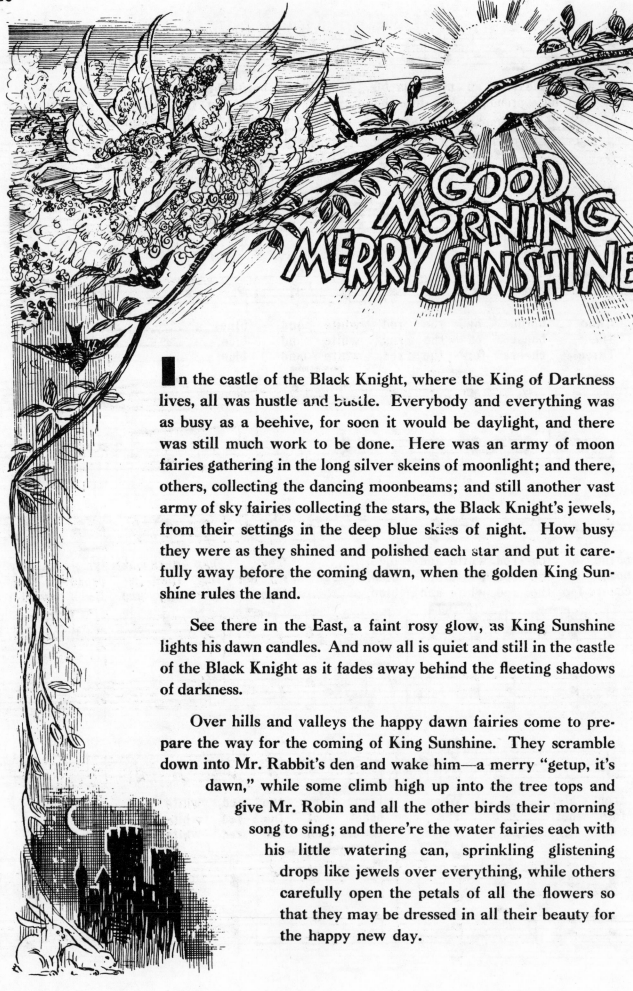

GOOD MORNING MERRY SUNSHINE

In the castle of the Black Knight, where the King of Darkness lives, all was hustle and bustle. Everybody and everything was as busy as a beehive, for soon it would be daylight, and there was still much work to be done. Here was an army of moon fairies gathering in the long silver skeins of moonlight; and there, others, collecting the dancing moonbeams; and still another vast army of sky fairies collecting the stars, the Black Knight's jewels, from their settings in the deep blue skies of night. How busy they were as they shined and polished each star and put it carefully away before the coming dawn, when the golden King Sunshine rules the land.

See there in the East, a faint rosy glow, as King Sunshine lights his dawn candles. And now all is quiet and still in the castle of the Black Knight as it fades away behind the fleeting shadows of darkness.

Over hills and valleys the happy dawn fairies come to prepare the way for the coming of King Sunshine. They scramble down into Mr. Rabbit's den and wake him—a merry "getup, it's dawn," while some climb high up into the tree tops and give Mr. Robin and all the other birds their morning song to sing; and there're the water fairies each with his little watering can, sprinkling glistening drops like jewels over everything, while others carefully open the petals of all the flowers so that they may be dressed in all their beauty for the happy new day.

Good Morning Merry Sunshine

Good morn-ing mer-ry sun-shine How did you wake so soon? You've
I nev-er go to sleep,dear, I just go 'round to see, My

scared the lit-tle stars a-way, And shined a-way the moon; I
lit-tle child-ren of the east, Who rise and watch for me; I

saw you go to sleep last night, Be-fore I ceased my play-ing, How
wak-en all the birds and bees, And flow-ers on my way, And

did you get 'way o-ver here, And where have you been stay-ing?
last of all the lit-tle child, Who stayed out late to play.

See - Saw

A. G. Crowe

See-saw, see-saw, now we're up___ or down,___ See-saw, see-saw, Now___ we're off to Lon-don Town.___ See-saw, see-saw, Boys and girls come out and play,___ See-saw,___ see-saw, On this our hol-i-day.

Made in U. S. A.

There's Pol - ly and John - ny and Kit - ty and Jane, All run - ning to get on the
Then come boys and girls and all join hands a - round, And mer - ri - ly skip with de -

see - saw a - gain, But Bob - by and Sal - ly al - read - y are there, And
light o'er the ground, Such frol - ic - some games ne'er be - fore have been seen, As

swing - ing the See - saw up high in the air. Ha ha, ha, ha, ha, ha, ha, ha,
we'll have to - day on the old vil - lage green.

ha, What! fun, ha, ha, ha, ha, ha, ha, ha, ha, ha, What fun!

Little Children's Day

Waking Or Sleeping

J . V . Blake

Wake, hap - py child - ren, In the dew - y morn, ___
Sleep, hap - py child - ren, In the ho - ly night, ___

Wake when the birds sing For the ro - sy dawn. ___
Gone is the sun - beam, But the stars are bright. ___

Wake at dawn wake at dawn Oh, _____
Sleep at night, sleep at night Oh, _____

Wake in_ the ro - sy dawn, Star - ry night is gone.
Sleep in_ the ho - ly night, When the stars are bright.

Made in U.S.A.

THE SANDMAN

It's getting late," says the Sandman as he looks at his clock, a funny old clock that tells the seconds and minutes and hours by the stars, the sun and the moon. "Yes, it's time for my journey," he remarks. So softly he calls to his sleep fairies to bring him his two magic bags, one filled with stardust and the other filled with dreams. Up they go, one over each shoulder, and swiftly he starts down to earth.

He comes around about the time when you are just a bit tired from playing all day and softly throws a little stardust into your eyes. And somehow, you just can't seem to keep them open. Sometimes, if you are bad and try to fool him and close your eyes just making believe you are going to sleep, he'll shake a little more stardust out of his magic bag and then, before you know it, you are off to Slumberland. The sandman smiles as he hums a lullaby and reaches into his other magic bag for dreams. Now, if you have been good all the day, he will leave beautiful, happy dreams; but if you have been bad, he may dig way to the bottom of his magic dream bag and leave a bad dream that will frighten you. No one has ever seen him, but sometimes at dusk you can hear the music of his lullabies echoing in the evening breeze, or in the dancing, tiny feet of the raindrops, as the Sandman rides by on the fleeting shadows at dusk.

The Sandman

J. L. Molloy

 Made in U.S.A.

Merrily We Sing

Im-prove the pass-ing hours For time is on the wing, Sip

hon-ey from the flow-ers, And mer-ri-ly, mer-ri-ly sing; All

fol-ly ends in sad-ness, For trou-ble it will bring; But

wis-dom leads to glad-ness, So mer-ri-ly, mer-ri-ly sing.

The Mill-Wheel

Copyright MCMXXXIV by Amsco Music Sales Co. New York City

Over The Summer Sea

G. Verdi

O - ver the sum-mer sea let our song gay and free ring in sweet mel-o - dy

sing-ing a hap-py song Hark to the birds on high. Sing 'neath a sum-mer sky

So let our hearts be free sing-ing sweet mel-o - dy Nev - er mind all sor - row

joy will come to - mor-row, Sing a hap-py song When ev-'ry-thing seems all right.

Made in U.S.A.

I Saw A Ship Sailing

Carl Reinecke

Spinning Song

Carl Reinecke

Spin, las - sie, spin, The
Sing, las - sie, sing, A

thread runs out and in. Grow - ing like your
mer - ry song to ring. As your spin - ning

gold - en hair, Know - ledge grows from year to year.
you be - gin Keep a cheer - ful heart with - in.

Spin, las - sie, spin, spin, las - sie spin.
Sing, las - sie, sing, sing, las - sie sing.

Made in U. S. A.

Song Of The Bells

R. Planquette

Daddy

F. Behrend

Take my head on your shoul-der Dad-dy, Turn your face to the west, It is
Why do your big tears fall_ Dad-dy, Moth-er's not far a-way, I_

just the hour when the sky turns gold, The hour that moth-er loves best The
of-ten seem to_ hear her voice, fall-ing a-cross my play And it

day has been long with-out you Dad-dy, You've been such a while a-way, And
some-times makes me cry_ Dad-dy, To think it's_ none of it true, Till I

now you're as tir'd of your work, Dad-dy, As I am tir'd of my play._ But
fall a_ sleep to dream, Dad-dy, Of home and moth-er and you._ For

Made in U.S.A.

I've got you and you've got me, So ev-'ry-thing seems right__ I
I've got you and you've got me, So ev-'ry-thing may go;__ We're

won-der if moth-er is think-ing of us, Be-cause it is my birth-day night.
all the world to each oth-er, dad, For moth-er once told me so

What Care We?

What care we for gold or sil-ver? What care we for house or land?

What care we for ships on the o-cean? On-ward go-ing hand in hand.

THE LITTLE TIN SOLDIER

JUST A LITTLE TIN SOLDIER, but how proud he was in his brand new uniform of red and gold that glistened in the light of the tiny lamp on the toymaker's work bench. His heart beat happily, for now his new clothes were dry and he was ready to join the rest of his regiment in a big cardboard box, and be sent out into the world of adventure.

He placed his trusty gun beside him and settled in his little niche in the box. Then came darkness; deep, pitch darkness, as the cover was fastened on his new home. He was not afraid, not a bit, for wasn't he a soldier? But he did set his gun a little closer to him as he made himself comfortable in his little resting place in the box, bravely awaiting his future.

Some days later he heard the rustle of paper, and bright daylight flooded his cardboard home and made the gay colors of his new uniform sparkle as he stood at attention. A happy child's voice greeted him as he was taken out of his box to parade for his new commander. And so for days and days, he paraded and fought, up and down, down and up, 'round and 'round and never a braver soldier wore a red and gold uniform.

But, one fatal day in a fierce play battle, he was charging up the long table when all of a sudden he stumbled and started to slide off the edge. He tried to hold on, but

the table was so hard and slippery—and then—oh—he fell from that terrible height, down, down, to the hard floor. He lay there in pain for quite awhile, and just as he was giving up hope he heard the child voice of his commander: "Gee, that's funny. There's one of my best soldiers missing" . . . and soon our little soldier was picked up and placed tenderly on the table. His red and gold uniform was chipped, but never a sound of complaint was heard from him, although something hurt him an awful lot, and he just couldn't move.

There were tears in his commander's eyes as he realized that never again would red and gold be able to join his regiment. "Oh, look," cried the child, "his leg is broken, his leg is broken." That was the last our little soldier heard, for he was so tired and sick he fell asleep. When he awoke, he was in a strange place all alone on the dusty top shelf of a toyshop, forgotten, lonely and broken-hearted; and so dreary hours stretched into long dreary days. One morning, as red and gold was rubbing the Sandman out of his sleepy eyes, he chanced to glance on the shelf below, and there he spied a strange new beautiful doll. She was so pretty in her bright silk dress and little golden curls stuck saucily out from under her cute bonnet. She glanced up at him and smiled, and his little heart went pit-a-pat, pit-a-pat, oh so fast, with happiness, and before he knew it he fell in love with her.

A few days later I came to see him, but he was gone. The dusty top shelf was empty, and as I stood there, wondering, a toy piano on the counter told me the rest of the story.

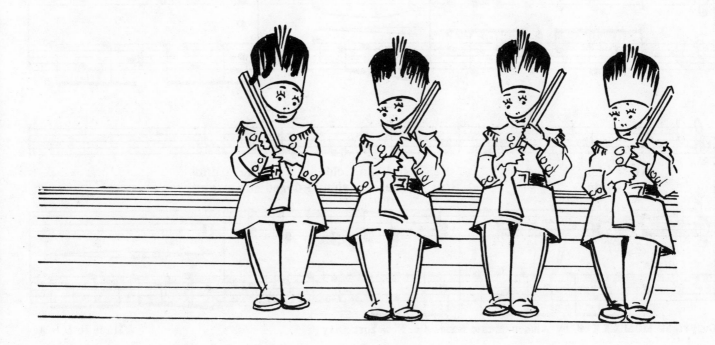

The Little Tin Soldier

F. E. Weatherly

J. L. Molloy

Made in U.S.A.

She was a dain - ty rose love, Far too grand for him,
Soon, ah, soon came the dark - ness, Life and love un - done,

He was a lit-tle tin sold - ier, One lit - tle leg had
He was a lit-tle tin sold - ier, One lit - tle leg had

he. Brave-ly shoul-der'd his mus - ket, Fain her love would

be. Soldiers marching up hill

he. Soldiers marching down hill

Once more he sees his rose love, Still she is danc-ing

gay, He is worn and fa-ded Loy-al still for

aye, Then came a hand that swept them

In - to a fur - nace wide, Part - ed in life, in dy - ing

They are side by side. Ah, for the lit - tle tin __ sol - dier,

Ah, for her cru - el part There lies her rose in ash - es,

There his loy - al lit - tle heart. __

I Love The Merry Sunshine

J. W. Lake

Stephen Glover

Made in U. S. A.

The Old Clock

Charles Swain

J. L. Molloy

voice, still strong, warned old and young, When the voice of friend-ship—
dawn look'd gray o'er the must - y way, And the air flew ver - y—

falt - er'd, Tick, tick! it said; Quick, quick to bed! For
cold - ly, Tick, tick! it said; Quick, out of bed! For

ten I've giv - en warn - ing, Up quick - ly and go, or
five I've giv - en warn - ing, You'll nev - er have health, you'll

sure - ly you know, You'll nev - er rise— soon in the morn - ing.
nev - er have wealth, Un - less you're up— soon in the morn - ing.

Ten Little Piggies

five lit - tle pig - gie pigs, Six lit - tle, seven lit - tle,
five lit - tle pig - gie pigs, Six lit - tle, seven lit - tle,

eight lit - tle, nine lit - tle, ten lit - tle pig - gie pigs.
eight lit - tle, nine lit - tle, ten lit - tle pig - gie pigs.

3

Six little piggies playing with a hive,

A bumble bee killed one,

And then there were five,

Five little piggies going in for law,

One got in chancery,

And then there were four.

4

Four little piggies going out to sea,

A red herring swallowed one,

And then there were three

Three little piggies walking in the zoo,

A big bear cuddled one

And then there were two.

5

Two little piggies sitting in the sun,

One got frizzled up,

And then there was one

One little piggie living all alone,

He got married

And then there were none.

6

One little piggie, with his little wife,

Lived all his days

A happy little life,

One little couple, dwelling by the shore,

Soon raised a family

Of two piggies more.

Chime Again, Beautiful Bells

Sir Henry Bishop

Chime a - gain, chime a - gain, beau - ti - ful bells, Now thy soft
Chime a - gain, chime a - gain, beau - ti - ful bells, Lin - ger a

mel - o - dy floats on the wind; Burst - ing at in - ter - vals
while o'er the deep dusk - y bay; Faint - er and faint - er thy

o - ver the sails, Leav - ing a train of re - flec - tion be - hind.
mel - o - dy swells, Fast fades the land and thy sounds die a - way.

Music Everywhere

S. W. Foster

Mu - sic in the val - ley, Mu - sic on the hill, Mu - sic in the
Mu - sic in the fire - side, Mu - sic in the hall, Mu - sic in the

Made in U. S. A.

wood - land, Mu - sic in the rill; Mu - sic on the moun - tain,
school - room, Mu - sic for us all; Mu - sic in our sor - row,

Mu - sic in the air, Mu - sic in the true heart, Mu - sic ev - 'ry - where.
Mu - sic in our care, Mu - sic in our glad - ness, Mu - sic ev - 'ry - where.

Little Things

Lit - tle drops of wa - ter, Lit - tle grains of sand, Make the might - y
And the lit - tle mo - ments, Hum - ble though they be, Make the might - y

o - cean And the beau - teous land, And the beau - teous land.
a - ges Of e - ter - ni - ty, Of e - ter - ni - ty.

 Made in U. S. A.

Sing, Gaily Sing

Sing gai-ly sing! Let glad-ness 'round us ring; This lit-tle, sim-ple,

cheer-ful lay, Shall be our part-ing song to-day. Sing gai-ly sing!

My Mother's Eyes

Carl Reinecke

In your eyes, O dar-ling moth-er, I could gaze the whole day long,
By my cra-dle, dar-ling moth-er, Thy dear eyes have watch'd o'er me,

See - ing in their love and kind-ness, All thy lov-ing lips would say.
While I rest in dream-ing slum-ber, Lulled to sleep by thy sweet song.

Made in U. S. A.

How Bright And Fair

G. Rossini

How bright and fair the morn__ is__ break-ing! We'll hail it with a__

mer - ry__ sound Of tune-ful chords, soft ech-oes waking, Or

notes that from far__hills re-bound; Of tune-ful chords, soft ech-oes wak-ing, Or

notes that from far hills re - bound; Then ply our work, just trib-ute mak - ing

Made in U.S. A.

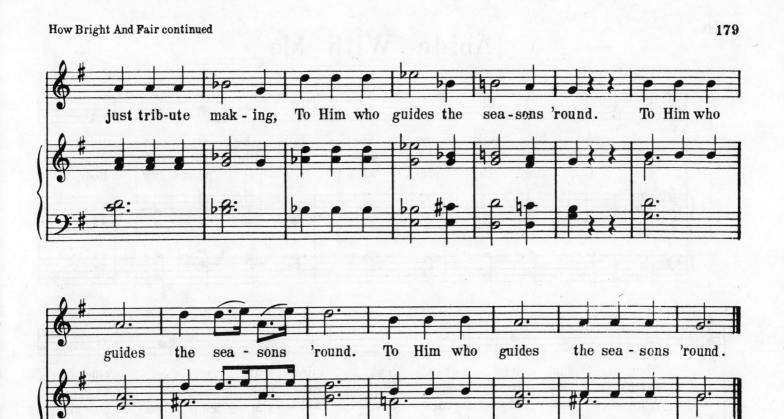

just trib-ute mak-ing, To Him who guides the sea-sons 'round. To Him who

guides the sea-sons 'round. To Him who guides the sea-sons 'round.

Good Night And Good Morning

A sweet lit-tle girl sat un-der a tree, A sew-ing as long as her eyes could see, Then
And while on her pil-low she soft-ly lay, She knew noth-ing more till a-gain 'twas day, And

smooth-ed her work and fold-ed it right, And said, "Dear work, good night good night.
all things said, in greet-ing the sun, "Good morn-ing, Good morn-ing our work is done.

Abide With Me

Slowly

W. H. Monk

A - bide with me Fast falls the e - ven tide,
Swift to its close, ebbs out life's lit - tle day;
I need Thy pres - ence ev - 'ry pass - ing hour,

The dark - ness deep - ens Lord, with me a - bide!
Earth's joys grow dim, its glo - ries pass a - way;
What but Thy grace can foil the temp - ter's pow'r!

When oth - er help - ers fail and com - forts flee,
Change and de - cay in all a - round I see;
Who, like Thy - self my guide and stay can be?

Help of the help - less oh, a - bide with me!
O Thou who chang - est not, a - bide with me!
Thro' cloud and sun - shine oh, a - bide with me!

Made in U.S.A.

Come, Thou Almighty King

Felice Giardini

Made in U. S. A.

Work, For The Night Is Coming

March Tempo

Lowell Mason

Work, for the night is com-ing, Work through the morn-ing hours;
Work, for the night is com-ing, Work through the sun-ny noon;
Work, for the night is com-ing, Un-der the sun-set skies;

Work while the dew is spark-ling, Work 'mid spring-ing flow'rs;
Fill bright-est hours with la-bor, Rest comes sure and soon;
While their bright tints are glow-ing, Work, for day-light flies;

Work when the day grows bright-er, Work in the glow-ing sun;
Give ev-'ry fly-ing min-ute, Some-thing to keep in store;
Work 'till the last beam fad-eth, Fad-eth to shine no more;

Work, for the night is com-ing, When man's work is done.
Work, for the night is com-ing, When man works no more.
Work, while the night is dark-'ning, When man's work is o'er.

Prayer

C. M. Von Weber

Slowly

Soft - ly sighs the voice of_ eve - ning,

Steal - ing through yon shad - y wil - low grove;

While the stars__ like guard - ian an - gels,

set their ho - ly_ night - ly watch a - bove

Lead Kindly Light

John Henry Newman

Rev. J. B. Dykes

Made in U. S. A.

Evening Prayer
(Hansel and Gretel)

E. Humperdinck

Made in U.S.A.

Sweet Hour Of Prayer

W.B.Bradbury

 Made in U.S.A.

Holy, Holy, Holy!

J. B. Dykes

Ho - ly, Ho - ly, Ho - ly! Lord___ God Al -
might - y! Ear - ly in the morn - ing our song shall rise to
thee; Ho - ly, Ho - ly, Ho - ly! mer - ci - ful and
might - y, God in three per - sons, bless - ed Trin - i - ty.

Made in U. S. A.

Nearer, My God, To Thee

Rock Of Ages

Thomas Hasting

Rock of a - ges cleft for me, Let me
Could my tears for - ev - er flow, Could my
While I draw this fleet - ing breath, When my

hide my - self in Thee; Let the wa - ter and the
zeal no lan - guor know, These for sin could not a -
eyes shall close in death, When I rise to worlds un -

blood, From thy wound - ed side which flowed, Be of
tone; Thou must save, and Thou a - lone: In my
known, And be - hold Thee on Thy throne, Rock of

sin the doub - le cure, Save from wrath and make me pure.
hand no price I bring; Sim - ply to Thy cross I cling.
a - ges cleft for me, Let me hide my - self in Thee.

Made in U. S. A.

Over The Stars There Is Rest

Fr. Abt

Old Hundred

(Doxology)

L. Bourgeois

Slowly

All peo-ple that on earth do dwell, Sing to the Lord with cheer-ful voice, Him
Know that the Lord is God in-deed; With-out our aid He did us make, We
Praise God, from whom all bless-ings flow, Praise Him all crea-tures here be-low; Praise

serve with mirth, His praise forth tell, Come ye be-fore Him and re-joice.
are His flock, He doth us feed, And for His sheep He doth us take.
Him a-bove, ye heav'n-ly host; Praise Fa-ther, Son, and Hol-ly Ghost.

Now The Day Is Over

J. Barnby

Now the day is o - ver, Night is draw-ing nigh,
Now the dark-ness gath - ers, Stars be-gin to peep,
Je - sus, give the wea - ry, Calm and sweet re - pose,

Shad - ows of the ev - 'ning Steal a - cross the sky.
Birds and beasts and flow - ers Soon will be a - sleep.
With Thy ten-d'rest bless - ing May our eye - lids close.

Now I Lay Me Down To Sleep

Now I lay me down to sleep, I pray the Lord my soul to keep, If

I should die be - fore I wake, I pray the Lord my soul to take.